Acoustic Guitar Hits

Alfred Music Publishing Co., Inc.

Los Angeles

International Standard Book Number: 978-0-7390-6705-5

Printed in the United States of America

Published under agreement by Alfred Music Publishing Co., Inc.

Distributed by Alfred Music Publishing Co., Inc. and Penguin Group (USA) Inc. All rights reserved.

Contributing Editor: *Andrew DuBrock*
Recordings: *Chauncey Gardiner Combo, featuring Erick Lynen on vocals*
Cover Photo: *Gibson Montana courtesy of Gibson Guitar Corp.*

Contents

Reviewing the Basics

Songs

Appendixes

Artist Index

Introduction

We all play guitar for pretty much the same reason—to play our favorite songs. It's so easy to get caught up in mastering technique, learning to read music, or understanding music theory, that we can spend hours at the instrument and still not have a good song to play. Note reading, technique, and theory are all great tools—but that's all they are. The focus of this book is to get you playing your favorite songs now! Playing your favorite songs is the single most important musical learning experience you can have. All the songs in this book use related chords, scales, techniques, and other elements, so as you learn your favorite songs, you are actually learning the skills you need to play other favorites as well.

Everything is included to help you play every song. First, there is a review of the basics, like holding the guitar and reading music and TAB. Every song is then presented with a short lesson that explores the tricks to making it easy to play. All the music is shown in standard music notation, TAB, and guitar chords so you can choose which is best for you. At the back of the book, there is a huge chord dictionary to help you play even more songs from sheet music and other books.

Most important are the recordings on the included CDs. Musicians learn by listening and imitating—the way a child learns to speak. Our included recordings allow you to learn in the most natural way possible—by listening and imitating. If you use the CDs in your CD player, you can hear sound-alike recordings of all the songs in the book. If you use the CDs in your computer and access the TNT software included on the discs, you can hear three versions of each song: a full-performance sound-alike recording, a version without vocals so you can hear the guitar parts more clearly, and a version without guitars so you can play along with the band. Listen to them often, and keep them handy as you learn each song. It's not important that you master every aspect of every song. You can focus on the parts that grab your attention the most—a lick you like, the melody, the chords, anything you *want* to play. As you gain experience, technique, and knowledge, putting the pieces together and learning the complete songs will get easier and easier. Also, the TNT software lets you loop sections for practice, slow tracks down or speed them up without changing the pitch, and even change the key. With so many tools at your disposal, you'll be able to nail any song you want in no time.

Be sure to check out the other books in this series to see if there are other favorites you'd like to learn. If you want more information on playing the guitar, reading music, or even writing your own music, there are lots of other *Complete Idiot's Guide*s to help you along.

Now tune your guitar, crank up your recordings, and dig in.

How to Use This Book

Some people approach learning an instrument by isolating all the technical skills, and, through years of study and practice, develop a command of those skills and tools. Others learn by having a friend show them a simple song, and then proceed to learn on a song-by-song basis. Some combination of the two methods is probably the best, but you should always spend a good portion of your music time learning songs that you would really love to perform for your friends and family—or for yourself.

In this book, each song is written in full music notation and TAB (tablature). Reading music is a skill acquired through diligent practice, and it has many benefits. But TAB offers a quick way of knowing what to play without having to be an accomplished music reader. We believe that providing TAB in conjunction with standard music notation is the ideal way to get you up and playing right away. Guitar chord grids indicate chord fingerings for strumming and fingerpicking accompaniment parts.

Start by picking a song you really want to play. Then listen carefully to the provided sound-alike recording (and the original version). Music is an aural art, so always have the sound of the song clearly in your head before you attempt to learn to play it on the guitar.

Read through the lesson that precedes each song and practice the music examples before attempting to play the whole song. Each lesson is broken into various sections. We've also included other info along the way to point out things that are particularly important, interesting, or helpful.

Steel Strings and Nylon Strings

Steel strings are found on both acoustic and electric guitars. They have a bright and brassy sound.

Nylon strings are usually found on classical and flamenco guitars. They have a mellow, delicate sound. **Nylon** strings tend to be easier on the fingers than steel strings.

How to Hold Your Guitar

Below are three typical ways of holding your guitar. Pick the one that is most comfortable for you.

Sitting.

Sitting with legs crossed.

Standing with strap.

Using Your Right Hand

Sometimes your right hand will play individual notes on a single string, and sometimes it will play chords using many strings. To *strum* means to play several strings by brushing quickly across them, either with a pick or with your fingers. This is the most common way of playing a chord.

Strumming with a Pick

Hold the pick between your thumb and index finger. Hold it firmly, but don't squeeze too hard.

On a *down-stroke*, strum from the lowest note of the chord to the highest note of the chord. Move mostly your wrist, not just your arm. For an *up-stroke*, strike the strings from highest to lowest.

TIP

Strumming is done mostly from the wrist, not the arm. Use as little motion as possible. Start as close to the string as you can, and never let your hand move past the edge of the guitar.

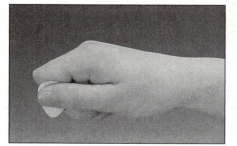

Holding the pick.

Starting near the lowest string.

Finishing near the highest string.

Strumming with Your Fingers

First, decide if you feel more comfortable strumming with the side of your thumb or with the nail of your fingers. The strumming motion is the same with the thumb or fingers as it is when using the pick.

Strumming with the thumb.

Strumming with the fingers.

Using Your Left Hand

Your left hand needs to be relaxed when you play. It's also important to keep your fingernails neat and trim so that your fingers will curve in just the right way, otherwise you'll hear lots of buzzing and muffling.

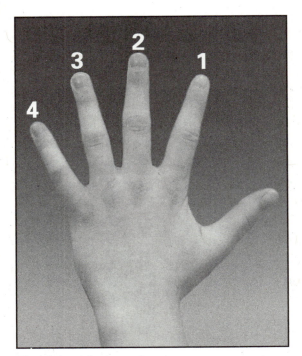

The left-hand finger numbers.

Proper Left-Hand Position

Your left-hand fingers will work best when your hand is correctly shaped and positioned. Place your hand so your thumb rests comfortably in the middle of the back of the neck and your wrist is away from the fretboard. Your fingers should be perpendicular to the fretboard.

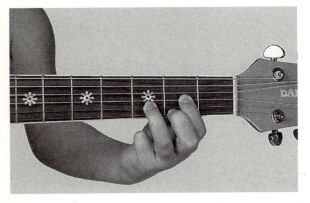

Front view.

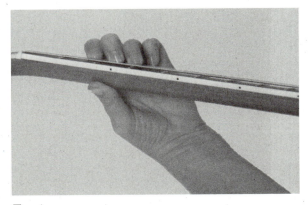

Top view.

Placing a Finger on a String

When you press a string with a left-hand finger, make sure you press firmly with the tip of your finger and as close to the fret wire as you can without actually being right on it. This will create a clean, bright tone. If your finger is too far from the fret wire, the note will buzz. If it is on top of the fret wire, you'll get a muffled, unclear sound. Also, make sure your finger stays clear of neighboring strings.

Right! The finger is close to the fret wire.

Wrong! The finger is too far from the fret wire.

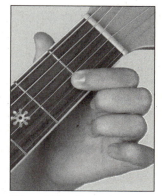

Wrong! The finger is on top of the fret wire.

Tuning Your Guitar

Every musician knows the agony of hearing an instrument that is not in tune. Always be sure to tune your guitar every time you play, and check the tuning every now and then between songs.

About the Tuning Pegs

First, make sure your strings are wound properly around the tuning pegs. They should go from the inside to the outside as shown in the illustration. Turning a tuning peg clockwise makes the pitch lower, and turning a tuning peg counter-clockwise makes the pitch higher. Be sure not to tune the strings too high, or you run the risk of breaking them.

TIP

Always remember that the thinnest, highest-sounding string, the one closest to the floor, is the *1st* string. The thickest, lowest-sounding string, the one closest to the ceiling, is the *6th* string. When guitarists say "the top string," they are referring to the highest-sounding string, and "the bottom string" is the lowest-sounding string.

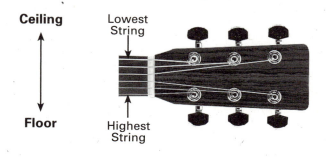

Ceiling

Floor

Lowest String

Highest String

Tuning Using the Included CDs

If you pop one of the included discs into your CD player, you'll notice that the first track is a tuning track. For your convenience, both CDs have the tuning track.

The first note plucked is the 1st string, and the track continues through the 2nd, 3rd, 4th strings, and so on. So one by one, make sure the pitches of the strings on your guitar match the notes you hear on the tuning track. Just adjust your tuning pegs accordingly. It may be difficult at first, but with practice and lots of attentive listening, it'll come naturally.

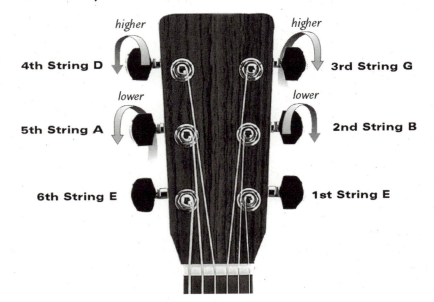

Tuning the Guitar to Itself

The day will surely come when your guitar is out of tune but you don't have your trusty play-along CDs with tuning tracks. If your 6th string is in tune, you can tune the rest of the strings using the guitar by itself. The easiest way to tune the 6th string is with a piano. If you don't have a piano available, consider buying an electronic tuner or pitch pipe. There are many types available, and a salesperson at your local music store can help you decide which is best for you.

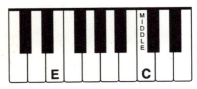

The 6th string is tuned to E below middle C.

If you have access to a piano, tune the 6th string to the note E below middle C.

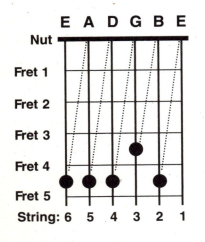

To tune the rest of the strings, follow this sequence:

- Press 5th fret of 6th string to get pitch of 5th string (A).
- Press 5th fret of 5th string to get pitch of 4th string (D).
- Press 5th fret of 4th string to get pitch of 3rd string (G).
- Press 4th fret of 3rd string to get pitch of 2nd string (B).
- Press 5th fret of 2nd string to get pitch of 1st string (E).

The Basics of Music Notation

Standard music notation contains a plethora of musical information. If you don't already read notation, you will probably benefit from studying the following fundamental concepts. Understanding even a little about reading notation can help you create a performance that is true to the original.

Notes

Notes are used to indicate musical sounds. Some notes are held long and others are short.

Note Values		
whole note	𝅝	4 beats
half note	𝅗𝅥	2 beats
quarter note	♩	1 beat
eighth note	♪	½ beat
sixteenth note	𝅘𝅥𝅯	¼ beat

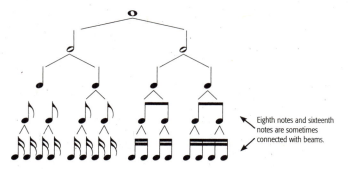

Eighth notes and sixteenth notes are sometimes connected with beams.

Relative note values.

When a *dot* follows a note, the length of the note is longer by one half of the note's original length.

Dotted Note Values		
dotted half note	𝅗𝅥.	3 beats
dotted quarter note	♩.	1 ½ beats
dotted eighth note	♪.	¾ beat

A *triplet* is a group of three notes played in the time of two. Triplets are identified by a small numeral "3" over the note group.

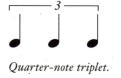

Quarter-note triplet.

Rests

Rests are used to indicate musical silence.

Rest Values		
whole rest	▬	4 beats
half rest	▬	2 beats
quarter rest	𝄽	1 beat
eighth rest	𝄾	½ beat
sixteenth rest	𝄿	¼ beat

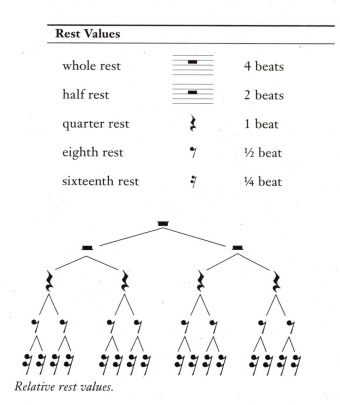

Relative rest values.

The Staff

Music is written on a *staff* made up of five lines and four spaces, numbered from the bottom up. Each line and space is designated as a different pitch.

line 5 →	← space 4
line 4 →	← space 3
line 3 →	← space 2
line 2 →	← space 1
line 1 →	

The staff is divided into equal units of time called *measures* or *bars*.

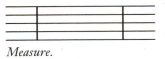

Measure.

A *bar line* indicates where one measure ends and another begins.

Bar line.

A *double bar line*, made of one thin line and one thick line, shows the end of a piece of music.

Double bar line.

Notes on the Staff

Notes are named using the first seven letters of the alphabet (A B C D E F G). The higher a note is on the staff, the higher its pitch.

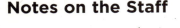

E F G A B C D E F

The *treble clef*, also called the *G clef*, is the curly symbol you see at the beginning of each staff. The treble clef designates the second line of the staff as the note G.

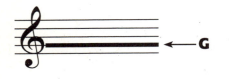

← G

Here are the notes on the lines of the treble staff. An easy way to remember them is with the phrase "Every Good Boy Does Fine."

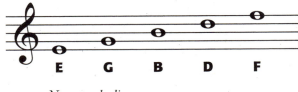

E   G   B   D   F

Notes on the lines.

Here are the notes on the spaces. They are easy to remember because they spell the word FACE.

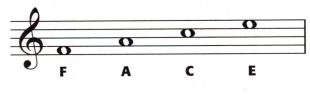

F   A   C   E

Notes on the spaces.

The staff can be extended to include even higher or lower notes by using *ledger lines*. You can think of ledger lines as small pieces of additional staff lines and spaces. The lowest note in the following figure is the open low E string of the guitar.

E F G A B C D G A B C

Notes on ledger lines.

Accidentals

An *accidental* raises or lowers the sound of a note. A *sharp* ♯ raises a note one *half step*, which is the distance from one fret to another. A *flat* ♭ lowers a note one half step. A *natural* ♮ cancels a sharp or a flat. An accidental remains in effect until the end of the measure, so if the same note has to be played flat or sharp again, only the first one will have the accidental. See the Guitar Fingerboard Chart on page 171 for all the flat and sharp notes on the guitar up to the 12th fret.

HALF STEPS • NO FRET BETWEEN

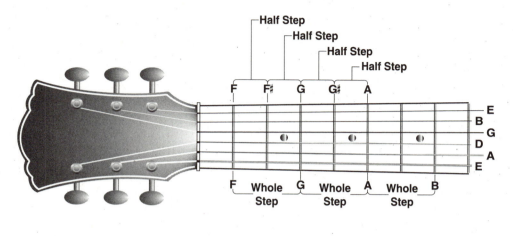

WHOLE STEPS • ONE FRET BETWEEN

Key Signatures

Sometimes certain notes need to be played sharp or flat throughout an entire song. In this case, it's easier to put the sharps or flats in the *key signature* instead of putting an accidental on each individual note. If you see sharps or flats at the beginning of a staff just after the treble clef, that means to play those notes sharp or flat throughout the music. The key signature can change within a song as well, so be sure to keep an eye out. Below are two examples of key signatures.

Play each F, C, and G as F♯, C♯, and G♯.

Play each B and E as B♭ and E♭.

Time Signatures

The *time signature* is a symbol resembling a fraction that appears at the beginning of the music. The top number tells you how many beats are in each measure, and the bottom number tells you what kind of note gets one beat. Most songs have the same number of beats in every measure, but the time signature can also change within a song. It's important to notice each time signature and count correctly, otherwise you could end up getting ahead in the song or falling behind.

$\frac{4}{4}$ Time

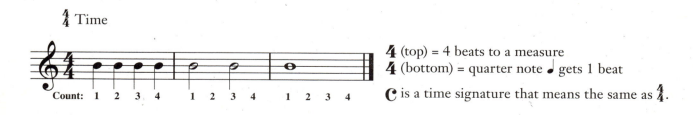

4 (top) = 4 beats to a measure
4 (bottom) = quarter note ♩ gets 1 beat

𝄴 is a time signature that means the same as $\frac{4}{4}$.

Count: 1 2 3 4   1 2 3 4   1 2 3 4

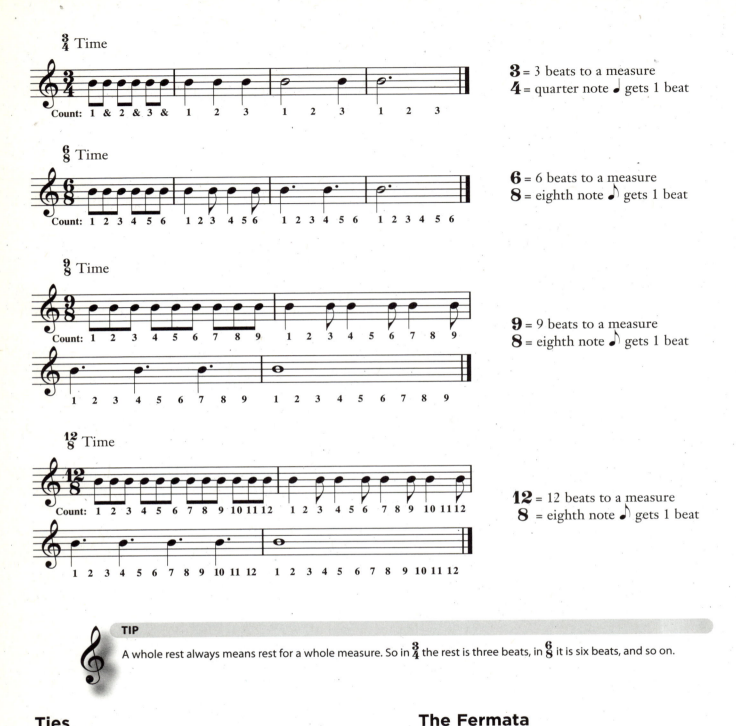

3 = 3 beats to a measure
4 = quarter note ♩ gets 1 beat

6 = 6 beats to a measure
8 = eighth note ♪ gets 1 beat

9 = 9 beats to a measure
8 = eighth note ♪ gets 1 beat

12 = 12 beats to a measure
8 = eighth note ♪ gets 1 beat

TIP

A whole rest always means rest for a whole measure. So in ¾ the rest is three beats, in ⁶⁄₈ it is six beats, and so on.

Ties

A *tie* is a curved line that joins two or more notes of the same pitch, which tells you to play them as one continuous note. Instead of playing the second note, continue to hold for the combined note value. Ties make it possible to write notes that last longer than one measure, or notes with unusual values.

Hold B for five beats.

The Fermata

A *fermata* 𝄐 over a note means to pause, holding for about twice as long as usual.

Pause on notes with a fermata.

Repeat Signs

Most songs don't start and then ramble on in one continuous stream of thought to the end. They are constructed with sections, such as verses and choruses, that are repeated in some organized pattern. To avoid having to go through pages and pages of duplicate music, several different types of *repeat signs* are used to show what to play over again. Repeat signs act as a kind of roadmap, telling you when to go back and where to go next, navigating you through the song.

Repeat Dots

The simplest repeat sign is simply two dots on the inside of a double bar. It means to go back to the beginning and play the music over again.

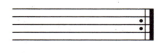

Go back and play again.

When just a section of music is to be repeated, an opposite repeat sign at the beginning of the section tells you to repeat everything in between.

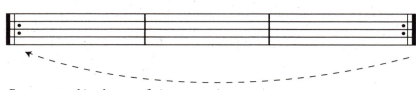

Repeat everything between facing repeat signs.

1st and 2nd Endings

When a section is repeated but the ending needs to be different, the *1st ending* shows what to play the first time, and the *2nd ending* shows what to play the second time. Play the 1st ending, repeat, then skip the 1st ending and play the 2nd ending.

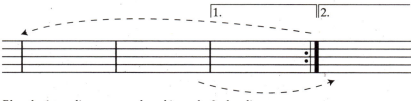

Play the 1st ending, repeat, then skip to the 2nd ending.

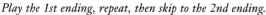

Other Repeat Signs

D.C. al Fine	Repeat from the beginning and end at ***Fine***.
D.C. al Coda	Repeat from the beginning and play to the coda sign ⊕, then skip to the ***Coda*** and play to the end.
D.S. al Fine	Repeat from the sign 𝄋 and end at ***Fine***.
D.S. al Coda	Repeat from the sign 𝄋 and play to the coda sign ⊕, then skip to the ***Coda*** and play to the end.

Reading Guitar Tablature (TAB)

Tablature, or *TAB* for short, is a graphic representation of the six strings of the guitar. Although standard notation tells you which notes and rhythms to play, the TAB staff tells you quickly where to finger each note on the guitar. The bottom line of the TAB staff represents the 6th string, and the top line is the 1st string. Notes and chords are indicated by the placement of fret numbers on each string.

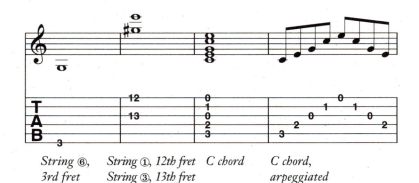

| *String ⑥,* | *String ①, 12th fret* | *C chord* | *C chord,* |
| *3rd fret* | *String ③, 13th fret* | | *arpeggiated* |

The following are examples of various guitar techniques you might come across in the notation of the songs. Unless otherwise indicated, the left hand does the work for these.

Bending Notes

Half step: Play the note and bend the string one half step (the sound of one fret).

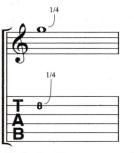

Slight bend/quarter-tone bend: Play the note and bend the string slightly sharp.

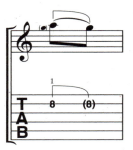

Prebend and release: Play the already-bent string, then immediately drop it down to the fretted note.

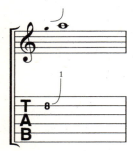

Whole step: Play the note and bend the string one whole step (the sound of two frets).

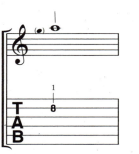

Prebend (ghost bend): Bend to the specified note before the string is plucked.

Unison bends: Play both notes and immediately bend the lower note to the same pitch as the higher note.

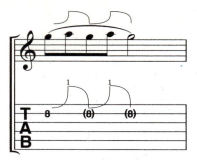

Bend and release: Play the note and bend to the next pitch, then release to the original note. Only the first note is attacked.

Bends involving more than one string: Play the note and bend the string while playing an additional note on another string. Upon release, relieve the pressure from the additional note, allowing the original note to sound alone.

Bends involving stationary notes: Play both notes and immediately bend the lower note up to pitch. Return as indicated.

Articulations

Hammer-on: Play the lower note, then "hammer" your left-hand finger onto the string to sound the higher note. Only the first note is plucked.

Muted strings: A percussive sound is produced by striking the strings with the right hand while laying the fret hand across them.

Pull-off: Play the higher note with your first finger already in position on the lower note. Pull your finger off the first note with a strong downward motion that plucks the string, sounding the lower note.

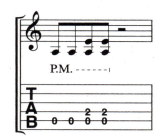

Palm mute: The notes are muted (muffled) by placing the palm of the right hand lightly on the strings, just in front of the bridge.

Legato slide: Play the first note, and with continued pressure applied to the string, slide up to the second note. The diagonal line shows that it is a slide and not a hammer-on or a pull-off.

Harmonics

Natural harmonic: Lightly touch the string with the fret hand at the note indicated in the TAB and pluck the string, producing a bell-like sound called a harmonic.

Artificial harmonic: Fret the note at the first TAB number, then use a right-hand finger to lightly touch the string at the fret indicated in parentheses (usually 12 frets higher than the fretted note), and pluck the string with an available right-hand finger or your pick.

Pick Direction

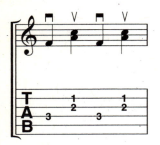

Down-strokes and up-strokes: The down-stroke is indicated with this symbol ⊓, and the up-stroke is indicated with this one ∨.

Rhythm Slashes

Strum marks with rhythm slashes: Strum with the indicated rhythm pattern. Strum marks can be located above the staff or within the staff.

Single notes with rhythm slashes: Sometimes single notes are incorporated into a strum pattern. The note name is given, with the string number in a circle and the fret number indicated.

Songs

Babe I'm Gonna Leave You

Key Thoughts

Led Zeppelin burned out of the gates with their eponymous debut in 1969. Heavy, riff-based songs held down a portion of the record, but the nuanced interplay between moody acoustic sections and thunderous interludes on "Babe I'm Gonna Leave You" hinted at their most-popular formula—one that peaked several years later with their hugest hit, "Stairway to Heaven."

Take Note

Pick the main acoustic guitar part with your thumb and fingers, using your thumb for the down-stemmed notes and your fingers for the up-stemmed ones. This rolling pattern, which uses each finger in ascending order, is a great way to get comfortable fingerpicking. Most chord shapes use your index, middle, and ring fingers on consecutive strings, but the trickier passages require you to spread your fingers and skip a string within the pattern, as seen in the opening measure (shown below). Also, notice the italic letters in between the notation and TAB in the example. These are often used for fingerpicking parts to show which fingers play which notes; thumb is *p*, index finger is *i*, middle is *m*, and ring is *a*. *Pima* notation will come in handy when you start playing more complex patterns.

FUN FACT

Bassist John Entwistle and drummer Keith Moon once tossed around the idea of forming a supergroup with Jimmy Page, and one of them joked that it would go over like a "lead zeppelin." Page liked the phrase so much that he used it as the name of his next band, spelling "led" to make sure nobody pronounced it with a long "e." Led Zeppelin didn't include Entwistle or Moon; Robert Plant sang lead vocals, John Bonham played the drums, and John Paul Jones held down the bass.

For the strummed section that starts in measure 33, either use your fingers as a group to strum the strings or put your index finger and thumb together to emulate a pick. To get the right feel, use downstrokes for the eighth notes and just one upstroke for the second sixteenth note in the first measure of the section (just before beat 2). The Dm(9)/A chord may look intimidating, but notice how it is just the Am chord shape slid up the neck.

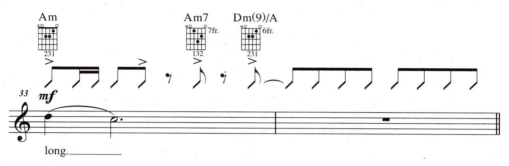

Near the end of the song (measures 126–127), Page's descending line requires a bit of a stretch, but that is the most efficient way to play it. If you find the stretch on the last two chords difficult, don't push it. Instead, try the alternate fingering below, which shifts your hand down to a lower position mid-way through the pattern.

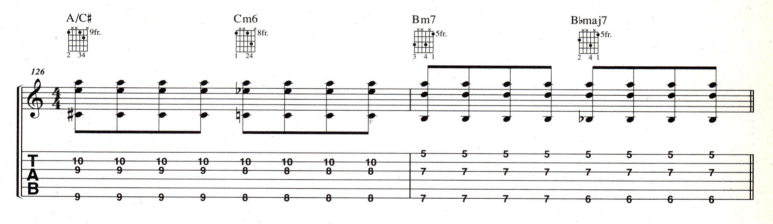

GUITAR GODS

Jimmy Page was already an accomplished guitarist by the time **LED ZEPPELIN** formed. Proficient at the age of 15, he was recruited to tour with The Crusaders. Later, while attending art school, Page found himself getting studio gigs, and he quickly established himself as a go-to studio guitarist. Add to this the groundbreaking work he did with the Yardbirds and Led Zeppelin, and it's no wonder Page is one of the most influential guitarists in rock music history.

Babe I'm Gonna Leave You

Words and Music by
ANNE BREDON, JIMMY PAGE
and ROBERT PLANT

Moderately bright, with a half-time feel ♩ = 134

1. Babe,
2.3. *See additional lyrics*

ba - by,   ba - by,___   I'm gon - na   leave   you.___

I   said,   ba - by,___   you

Interlude:

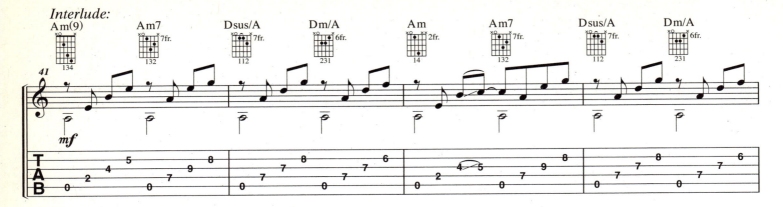

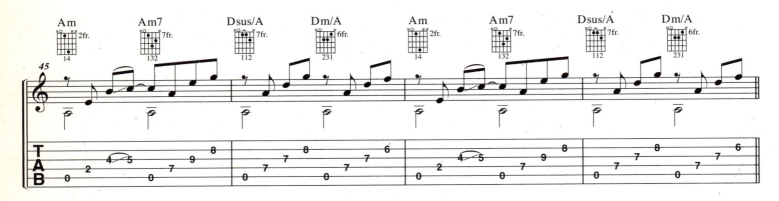

Bridge:

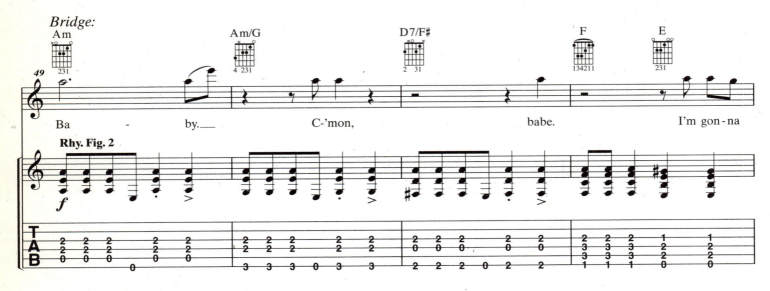

D.C. al Coda

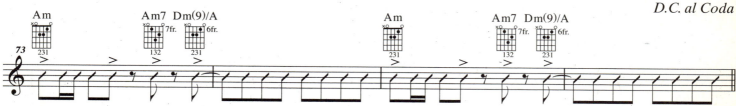

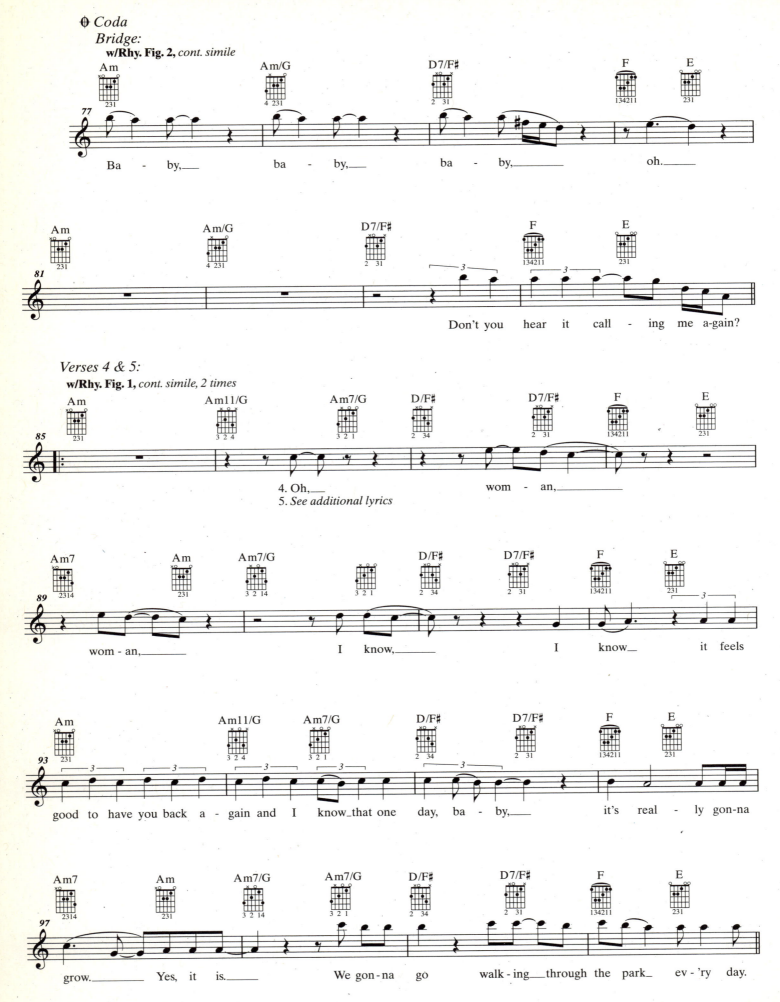

*Unison E notes played on 1st and 2nd strings.

Verse 2:
Babe, babe, babe, babe, babe, babe, baby,
Mmm, baby, I wanna leave you,
I ain't joking, woman, I've got to ramble.
I can hear it calling me the way it used to do.
I can hear it calling me back home.
(To Bridge:)

Verse 3:
I know, I know, I know I'm never, never, never, never,
Never gonna leave you, babe.
But I got to go away from this place.
I got to quit you, yeah.
Oh, baby, baby, baby, baby.
(To Bridge:)

Verse 5:
Oh, miss your lips, sweet baby.
It was really, really good.
You made me happy ev'ry single day.
But now I've got to go away.
Baby, baby, baby, baby.
(To Outro:)

Black Water

Key Thoughts

By the time they released *What Were Once Vices Are Now Habits* in 1974, The Doobie Brothers had already tasted success with "Listen to the Music," "China Grove," and "Long Train Runnin'." But "Black Water" eclipsed these three great songs, providing the band with its first No. 1 hit and propelling *What Were Once Vices Are Now Habits* up to No. 4 on *Billboard*'s top 200 album chart.

Take Note

The really cool acoustic guitar part for "Black Water" uses *Double Drop D tuning*. Sounds complicated, but it's not. Just tune your 1st string (high E) down a whole step to D (match it to the 3rd fret of your 2nd string). Then tune your 6th string (low E) down a whole step to D. Make sure to pluck your retuned 1st string so you can hear when the low string is in tune; the two strings will ring in tune together.

The song transcription uses two methods for notating the fingerpicked acoustic guitar part: with notes combined on single stems, such as in measures 1–4, and with split stems, such as in measures 13–18.

The opening figure is simply one part played fingerstyle with the thumb and fingers, so it's notated with single stems. Split stems, however, show when two parts are being played at the same time; for example, at bar 13, the thumb is playing a bass line (down-stems), while the fingers are playing melodic chordal fills (up-stems). The split stems are also used to separate what the thumb is playing from what the fingers are playing; the thumb usually handles all the down-stem notes, while the fingers play all the up-stem notes. (But note that split stems can make music look more complicated, so when it's a question of readability, single stems are often the choice.)

FUN FACT

The Doobie Brothers had several distinct phases over the course of their career, and their two most popular incarnations sounded like completely different bands. The first of these lineups featured Tom Johnston and Patrick Simmons singing and writing songs. "Black Water" comes from this era, as well as "China Grove" and "Listen to the Music." Due to health issues, Johnston took a diminished role in the band, and his replacement, Michael McDonald, became the face of their other popular phase—providing the sonic change via his distinctive vocal style and keyboard playing. Songs from this era include "What a Fool Believes," "Takin' It to the Streets," and "Minute by Minute."

At measure 13, if you grab the G chord with your ring and pinky fingers, you can access the other notes on the 1st string with your index finger. Notice the tricky move on the following B♭ chord on the "&" of beat 2—where you lift your pinky off of the 7th fret and play the 7th-fret A note with your middle finger.

Measures 19–22 (and measure 25) return to the single-stem approach. For a similar split-stem version, see below.

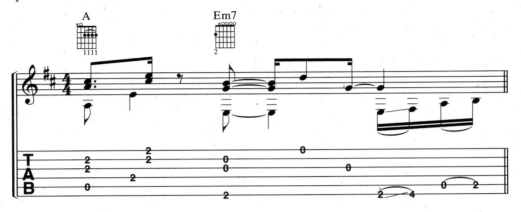

Here's a split-stem version of the D5–Am7(4) chord progression (measures 23–24):

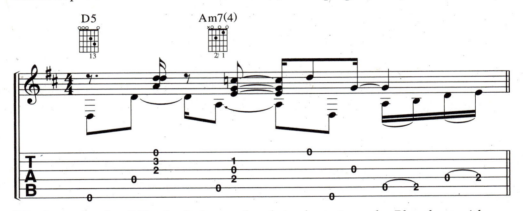

Watch out for the difficult whole-step bends in the guitar solo. Play them with your ring finger, backing that up with your index and middle fingers. Also look out for the double-stop 6th run in measures 38–39 (on the 1st and 3rd strings). Pay attention to the fret numbers here, since notes along the 1st string will be two frets higher (due to the tuning).

TIP

If you have trouble playing the whole-step bends in the guitar solo, try replacing your 3rd string with an unwound string. An unwound string has less tension, and you'll have an easier time pushing the string up a whole step.

Black Water

Acous. Gtr. 1 in Dbl. Drop D tuning:

⑥ = D ③ = G
⑤ = A ② = B
④ = D ① = D

Words and Music by
PATRICK SIMMONS

Outro:

w/Rhy. Fig. 1 *(Acous. Gtr. 1) cont. simile till fade*

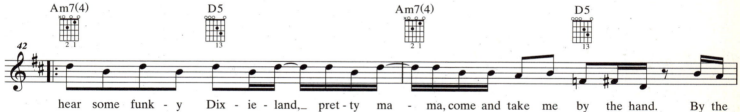

hear some funk - y Dix - ie - land,_ pret - ty ma - ma, come and take me by the hand. By the
*Acous. Gtr. 1 fades out and then fades back in.

Repeat ad lib. and fade

hand, take me by the hand, pret-ty ma-ma, come and dance with your dad-dy all__ night long. I'd like to

Verse 2:
Well, if it rains, I don't care,
Don't make no difference to me;
Just take that streetcar that's goin' uptown.
Yeah, I'd like to hear some funky
Dixieland and dance a honky-tonk,
And I'll be buyin' everybody drinks all 'round.
(To Chorus:)

Big Yellow Taxi

Key Thoughts

Joni Mitchell has become one of the world's foremost proponents of *altered tunings*. An altered tuning is simply a different way of tuning one or more strings. Although playing in an altered tuning can be disorienting at first, it can also open the door to easy creative explorations and lead the way to new sonic possibilities on the guitar.

Take Note

"Big Yellow Taxi," from relatively early in Joni's career, is in *Open E tuning*. In Open E, each string on the guitar is tuned to one of the notes of an E major chord. Joni represents this tuning as E–7–5–4–3–5. This system tells you that the low 6th string is tuned to E, the open 5th string is tuned to the 7th of the 6th string, the open 4th string is tuned to the 5th fret of the 5th string, and so on.

Using open tunings on the guitar can present challenges, but can also create opportunities. One major plus is that you can produce a chord simply by barring your finger across the fretboard in any position. Another advantage is that you can take the "conventional" chord fingerings from standard tuning and use them in an altered tuning to reveal delightful combinations of notes that would have been inconceivable in standard tuning.

Open E tuning.

DEFINITION

When you tune your guitar's strings to anything other than standard tuning, you're in an **altered tuning**. There are countless altered tunings, and some of the most popular include Drop D tuning and DADGAD. If you're tuned to the notes of any major or minor chord, you're in an **open tuning**. Along with the Open E tuning used in "Big Yellow Taxi," other popular tunings include Open G and Open D.

"Big Yellow Taxi" has three basic chords: E, A, and B, played in the open, 5th-fret, and 7th-fret positions, respectively, with an occasional embellishment on the open E chord. Happy strummin'!

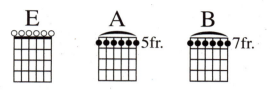

FUN FACT

The first "Earth Day" was in 1970, the same year this song was published. At the dawn of the environmental movement, Joni Mitchell came up with this simple, light-hearted tune with a whimsical warning: "They paved paradise and put up a parking lot."

TIP

Tuning your guitar up to Open E places a lot of tension on the strings. You might even break a string. So instead of tuning up, many guitarists tune down to Open D—the exact same tuning as Open E, but down a whole step. Then you can just place a capo at the 2nd fret to match the key of the recording. Open D: D–A–D–F♯–A–D

Big Yellow Taxi

Acous. Gtr. in Open E tuning:
⑥ = E ③ = G♯
⑤ = B ② = B
④ = E ① = E

Words and Music by
JONI MITCHELL

Verse 2:
They took all the trees,
Put 'em in a tree museum.
And they charged the people
A dollar and a half just to see 'em.
(To Chorus:)

Verse 3:
Hey farmer, farmer,
Put away that DDT now.
Give me spots on my apples,
But leave me the birds and the bees,
Please!
(To Chorus:)

Verse 4:
Late last night
I heard the screen door slam.
And a big yellow taxi
Took away my old man.
(To Chorus:)

Coconut

Key Thoughts

Harry Nilsson's quirky pop style was at its peak when he released *Nilsson Schmilsson* in 1971. The record showed off Nilsson's eclectic influences, and produced three hits, all of which sounded like they were written by completely different artists: the melodramatic chart topper "Without You," the rocking and rollicking "Jump into the Fire," and the offbeat "Coconut." While "Without You" was the Grammy winner and No. 1 hit, "Coconut" has endured as a cult favorite. The song's island-music sound, paired with what sounds like a recipe for a hangover cure, has made it a party favorite to this day. On the recording, Ian Duck plays the central acoustic guitar part, while Caleb Quaye adds electric guitar licks.

Take Note

"Coconut" revolves around a single C7 chord fingerpicked throughout the whole song. If you check out the C7 chord shape in the example below, you'll notice that the low G note on the 6th string isn't part of this shape, even though it's in the notation and TAB on beat 3. To access that note, lift your 3rd finger off of the 5th string and place it on the 3rd fret of the 6th string, making sure to keep the rest of the C7 chord fretted. As you approach the beginning of the next measure, move your 3rd finger back to grab the C note on the 5th string. Practice this move until the switch between the 5th and 6th strings feels like a natural, rocking motion.

Pick the down-stemmed notes with your thumb (*p*), and try using your index (*i*), middle (*m*), and ring (*a*) fingers on the 4th, 3rd, and 2nd strings, respectively (as shown below). If you're not comfortable using your ring finger for picking, use your index finger for the third and fifth notes (the E and the final B♭) and your middle finger for the other three notes.

At the second verse, guitarist Caleb Quaye adds *double stops* over the top of Ian Duck's acoustic guitar part. (For a definition of double stops, see the performance notes to "Hey There Delilah" on page 64.) Barre your ring finger across the 2nd and 3rd strings at the 10th fret for the first double stop. Then, barre across the 8th fret with your index finger for the second double stop, and quickly hammer onto the 9th fret with your ring finger after picking the notes.

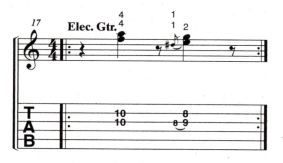

  TIP

Don't let the placement of the grace note (that small note with a line through its flag) in the electric guitar lick throw you off. It may look like it happens *before* the following double-stop quarter note, but it actually happens *simultaneously* with the 8th-fret G.

FUN FACT

Harry Nilsson was a well-respected songwriter whose songs are covered by a host of other musicians, like John Lennon, the Monkees, Glen Campbell, and Three Dog Night (who had a huge hit with Nilsson's "One"). Ironically, two of Nilsson's biggest hits were written by other artists: "Without You" was penned by Badfinger, and "Everybody's Talkin'" was written by Fred Neil.

Coconut

Moderately fast ♩ = 134

Words and Music by
HARRY NILSSON

43

drink 'em both to - geth - er, put the lime in the co - co - nut then___ you'll feel___ bet - ter. Put the

46

lime in the co - co - nut, drink 'em both___ up. Put the lime in the co - co - nut and

Bridge:

49

call me in the morn - ing. Woo,___ woo,___ oo, woo,___ oo,___ oo.___

Elec. Gtr.

52 *Elec. Gtr. cont. simile*

Woo,___ woo,___ oo, oo, oo, oo, oo.___ Woo,___ woo,___

55

oo,___ oo,___ oo,___ oo,___ oo,___ oo,___ oo,___ oo.

Verse 4:

58

Broth - er bought a co - co - nut, he bought it for a dime. His sis - ter had an - oth - er one, she paid it

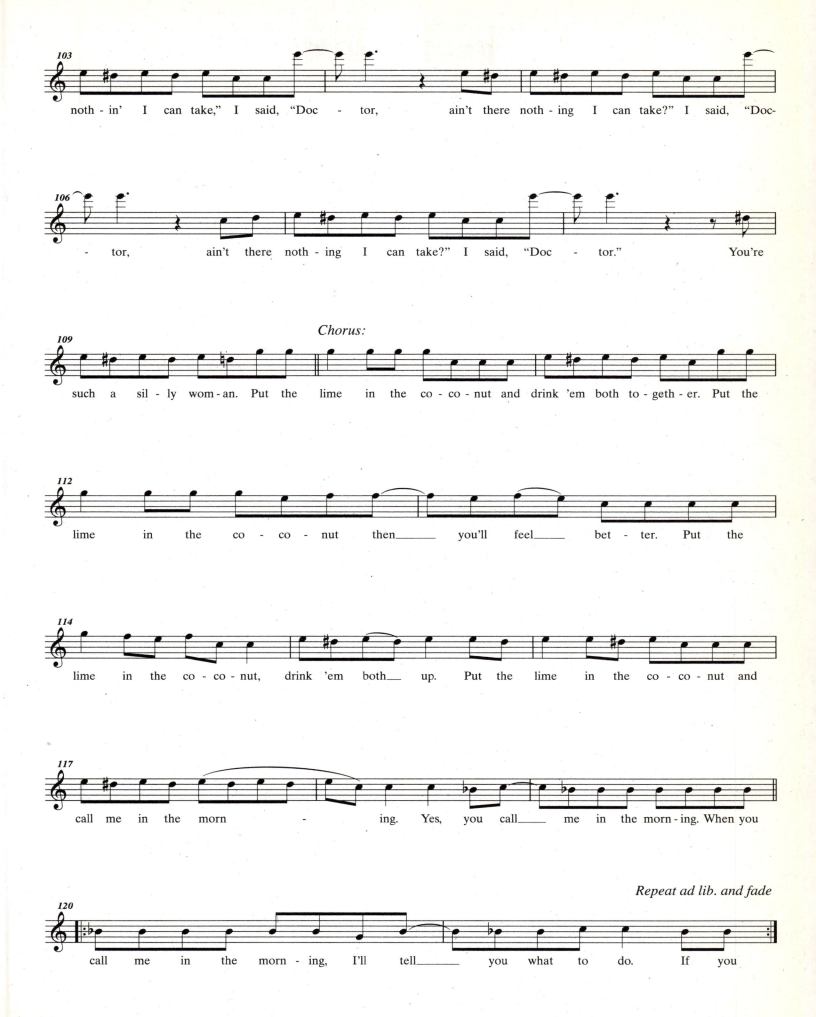

Danny's Song

Key Thoughts

"Danny's Song" is a tune that Kenny Loggins performed with Loggins & Messina. The basic fingerpicking accompaniment is a simplified *Travis picking* pattern, and learning this song is great preparation for playing songs with more complex Travis patterns. (For more on Travis picking with another great song example, see Fleetwood Mac's "Never Going Back Again," on page 132.)

Take Note

The first thing to work on is understanding the correct rhythmic *groove*, or feel. Without the right groove, the song just won't feel right. Notice the time signature at the beginning of the first measure; it's a "C" with a slash through it ₵. This symbol means *cut time*. Cut time is $\frac{2}{2}$: two beats per measure, and a half note gets one beat. To get into this feel, tap your foot at a medium tempo *two* times per measure, not four. That means each grouping of four eighth notes is played in the space of one foot tap. Now place a slight accent (stress) on the last note of each four-note group, allowing that note to ring out a little bit more than the others. Once you do that, the accent patterns will automatically change, and you'll be grooving right.

Now we're ready to work on the fingerpicking pattern. Most Travis patterns are more complex than the one in this song, and our version is even slightly simplified from how Kenny Loggins actually performs it. To play this pattern, your thumb needs to constantly alternate between two strings on each quarter-note beat. The thumb notes are indicated with down-stems in the notation. In between the thumb strokes, just alternate using your index and middle fingers. Try the D chord pattern shown below.

We have two important fingerings to point out. First, when transitioning from the D chord to the C(9), keep your 3rd finger locked on the 2nd-string D at the 3rd fret. That will be your pivot point. Since that note is common to both chords, continue to hold it while your other fingers move to play the C(9) chord.

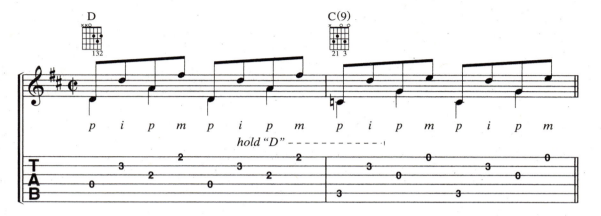

The other fingering is on the A chord in measures 9 and 10. Look at the example below, and you'll see that a little melody is created by changing the last note of each four-note group. The melody is C♯–D– E. To play this, hold the A chord, then slide your 3rd finger up to D at the end of measure 9 and keep it there. The E is the open 1st string, so you can continue holding your 3rd finger on D through bar 10 and again use it as a pivot point to transition back to the D chord in measure 11.

FUN FACT

Jim Messina, a very experienced guitarist and producer, was originally hired to produce the first record by a very young Kenny Loggins. The pairing was so successful, however, that the record label asked them to tour and perform as a duo—and Loggins & Messina was born.

Danny's Song

Words and Music by
KENNY LOGGINS

you bring a tear of joy___ to my eyes,___ and tell me___ ev - 'ry -

[1.2.3.] D.S. 𝄋 [4.] D.S. 𝄋 al Coda

- thing___ is gon-na be al - right.___   - thing___ is gon-na be al - right.___

⊕ Coda

Verse 3:
Pisces, Virgo rising is a very good sign,
Strong and kind,
And the little boy is mine.
Now I see a family where there once was none.
Now we've just begun,
Yeah, we're going to fly to the sun.
(To Chorus:)

Verse 4:
Love the girl who holds the world in a paper cup.
Drink it up,
Love her and she'll bring you luck.
And if you find she helps your mind, better take her home,
Don't you live alone, try to earn what lovers own.
(To Chorus:)

Cat's in the Cradle

Key Thoughts

"Cat's in the Cradle" was Harry Chapin's most commercially successful song, reaching No. 1 on the pop charts in December of 1974—not a bad achievement for a man whose ambitions did not originally lie in songwriting. The lyrics were derived from a poem penned by his wife, Sandy, and tell the poignant tale of a father so consumed with work that he finds no time for his son. Eventually, the son grows up and is unwilling to make time for his father, turning the tables on the old man who realizes too late, "My boy was just like me."

Take Note

The original recording of "Cat's in the Cradle" employs a capo on the 8th fret. The fingerpicking pattern in the intro and first three verses includes an alternating bass played with the thumb in a style commonly known as Travis picking. (For a detailed explanation of the Travis picking technique, see the notes for the song "Never Going Back Again," on page 132.) Use your thumb to keep a steady pulse on all of the down-stem notes, and once you're comfortable with that, begin introducing the notes with up-stems.

Notice that a basic strum pattern of quarter-note downstrokes is introduced in the chorus. Fingerpicking resumes on the second and third verses, but from the third chorus to the end, everything is strummed.

GUITAR GODS

Singer-songwriter **HARRY CHAPIN** was an artist with many talents. While in high school, he formed a band and sang in a boys' choir, but it was actually a career in documentary filmmaking, not music, that he pursued in college. He found almost immediate success when a film he directed, *Legendary Champions,* received a nomination for an Academy Award. The music world was fortunate, though, when Chapin decided to switch careers a few years later. His first foray into music came in the summer of 1972 with the release of his debut album, *Heads and Tails.* It included the hit song "Taxi," which soon became one of his signature tunes. Chapin's most successful album, *Verities & Balderdash,* was released two years later. Featuring his biggest hit song, "Cat's in the Cradle," the album peaked at No. 4 on the U.S. charts and went on to become a gold record. Shortly after the album's release, Chapin branched off into further artistic exploration and began working on a musical, *The Night That Made America Famous,* which earned two Tony nominations. Tragically, the life of this diverse and beloved artist was cut short by an auto accident in 1981.

Cat's in the Cradle

Capo 8th fret to match recording.

Words and Music by
HARRY CHAPIN and SANDY CHAPIN

𝄋 *Verses 1–3:*

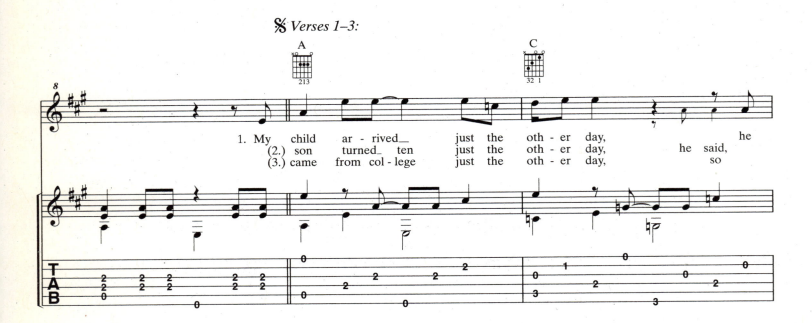

1. My child ar - rived__ just the oth - er day,   he
(2.) son turned__ ten just the oth - er day, he said,
(3.) came from col - lege just the oth - er day,   so

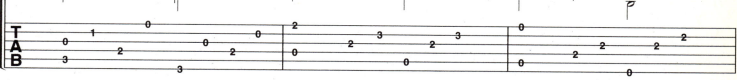

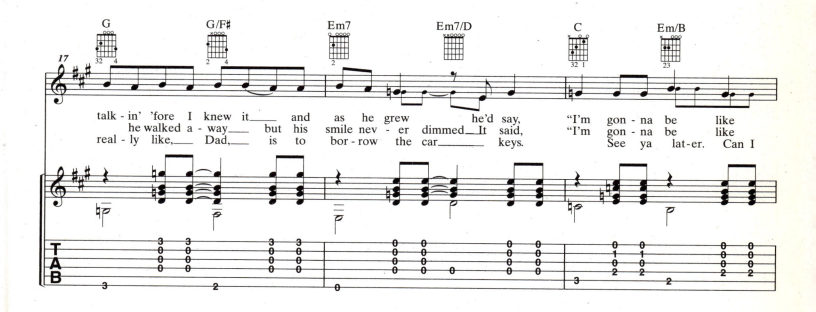

For What It's Worth

"For What It's Worth" was Buffalo Springfield's first—and biggest—single. Reaching No. 7 on the Billboard Hot 100 chart, the tune documents several late-1960s riots on the Sunset Strip and became one of the signature songs of the decade. While some think the song was a reaction to the 1970 Kent State University shootings, the song was actually released in late 1966—almost four years earlier.

"For What It's Worth" starts with several electric guitar *harmonics* played over strummed root-position acoustic guitar chords. (If you need assistance playing these harmonics, see the tip for "She Talks to Angels" on page 121.) At the end of the second measure, another acoustic guitar enters with a riff. You may naturally want to start this lick by using your index finger for the second note, but if you do this, the slide will put your hand out of place for the rest of the riff. Instead, use your ring finger for that note, and your index finger will then be in place to fret the next note—that 2nd-fret E on the 4th string.

DEFINITION

Those small notes at the beginning of each slide in this song are called **grace notes.** Grace notes are notes played very quickly either just before a beat or right on the beat. This means that, here, you'll need to perform your slide immediately after plucking the note.

As you strum through Gtr. 2's part on the verse, use the strum pattern shown in measures 5–6, and continue with a similar pattern. Note the A7 chords in parentheses; add these chords during verses 3 and 4.

FUN FACT

Buffalo Springfield was formed on a chance encounter in Los Angeles, when Stephen Stills was driving down Sunset Boulevard with Richie Furay and spotted a hearse driving the other way. Stills had crossed paths with Neil Young earlier in Canada, and he recognized the hearse as Young's. After flagging down Young and his passenger, Bruce Palmer, the collective group decided they should start a band.

GUITAR GODS

Both Neil Young and Stephen Stills are accomplished guitarists. Sharing duties in **BUFFALO SPRINGFIELD** and their other supergroup, Crosby, Stills, Nash & Young, the two also carved out successful solo careers. Young became one of the biggest icons of the 20th century, appealing to a broad audience by virtue of his divergent sounds. His poetic, acoustic songs appealed to folk fans, and his seat-of-the-pants electric guitar work with Crazy Horse made him a hero in heavier circles (where he's sometimes referred to as the "father of grunge" music).

For What It's Worth

Words and Music by
STEPHEN STILLS

Verse 2:
There's battle lines being drawn,
Nobody's right if everybody's wrong.
Young people speaking their minds,
Getting so much resistance from behind.
I think it's time we stop,...
(To Chorus:)

Verse 3:
What a field day for the heat,
A thousand people in the street.
Singing songs and carrying signs,
Mostly say, "Hooray for our side."
It's time we stop,...
(To Chorus:)

*Verse 4:
Paranoia strikes deep,
Into your life it will creep.
It starts when you're always afraid,
Step out of line, the man come and take you away.
We better stop,...
(To Chorus:)

Good Riddance
(Time of Your Life)

American punk band Green Day struck a mellow, reflective pose with "Good Riddance (Time of Your Life)." Released in the period between the band's 1994 breakout success and their 2004 rise to mega-superstar status with *American Idiot*, this introspective acoustic ballad (with strings!) was a 180-degree about-face for the band heretofore known for edgy hard-driving rock.

Billie Joe Armstrong plays the guitar on "Good Riddance" in a casual, arpeggiated fashion. Note that, while holding the G5 chord position, the left-hand 2nd finger extends up to the 3rd fret of the 6th string, muting the 5th string in the process. Strum down with a pick, emphasizing the bass strings, then repeat the down-strum and quickly follow it with an up-stroke across the 2nd and 3rd strings together. Next, individually pick open strings 3, 4, and 3 using
up-stroke, down-stroke, up-stroke (respectively), and you've got the basic arpeggio pattern of the introduction, first verse, and chorus. Try it slowly at first, and gradually build up speed until you can play along with the recording without a second thought.

TIP

See how the 3rd finger remains stationary on the 3rd fret of the 2nd string for the first three chords (G5, Csus2, D5)? Don't move that finger. Keep it planted firmly in place, and try to minimize the movement of your fingers at all times. As a general rule, when two sequential chords share a note, try not to remove that finger from the fretboard as you transition from one chord to the next; you'll be able to make the chord changes smoothly and quickly that way.

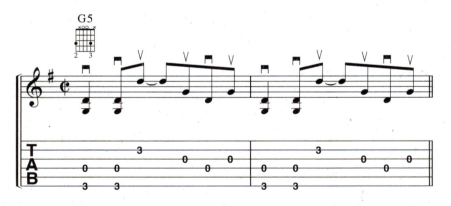

From measure 27 in the chorus to the 3rd ending, you have the option of strumming the chords, arpeggiating each chord throughout, or breaking the monotony and giving the performance more dynamic interest by picking one part and strumming rhythm on another. When strumming, use the pattern below. Notice that full chords are used in this option, not the "5" and sus2 chords employed in the arpegiatted introduction. Similar to the picked pattern at the beginning, you should emphasize the bass strings of each chord with a down-stroke on beat 1 of each measure. Note the *accent* > on beat 2, which tells you to strum all the notes of the chord with more force on that beat.

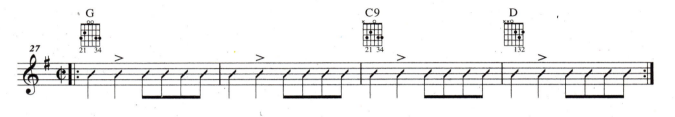

To finish, resume the intro arpeggios for a return to a softer style at the 3rd ending.

 FUN FACT

"Good Riddance (Time of Your Life)" was featured over a retrospective montage on the final episode of *Seinfeld* in 1998.

Good Riddance
(Time of Your Life)

Lyrics by BILLIE JOE
Music by BILLIE JOE and GREEN DAY

Hey There Delilah

Key Thoughts

"Hey There Delilah," by the Plain White T's, first appeared in 2005 as the final track on the band's second record, *All That We Needed*. But the song didn't take off until 2007 when an updated version was released as a single, climbed the charts, and turned the Plain White T's into instant stars.

While the Plain White T's are best known for this song and another acoustic-driven tune, "1, 2, 3, 4," most of their songs feature upbeat rhythms and a crunchy, power-pop sound.

Take Note

Play "Hey There Delilah" with your thumb and fingers, picking out the notes indicated in the notation and TAB. Use your thumb for the lower notes on each beat, and grab the *double stops* (two-note chords) on the offbeats with your index and middle fingers. The example below uses traditional pick-hand labeling: *p* = thumb, *i* = index, and *m* = middle. These abbreviations come from the Spanish terms for each finger: *p* = pulgar, *i* = indice, *m* = medio.

DEFINITION

A **double stop** is any two fretted notes played together (double = two strings; stop = stopping a string). The term likely came from the classical music world via the fretless stringed instruments—like violin and viola—where your fingers, not the frets, actually "stop" the strings by pressing them into the fretboard.

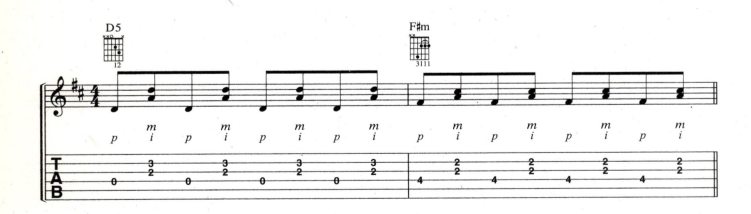

For the most part, once your pick-hand fingers are in place, they'll pluck the same notes throughout each chord's duration. Occasionally, though, you'll need to grab a different bass note with your thumb, as seen in the first measure of the chorus, shown below. Sometimes the bass note moves, which means you'll need to adjust your fret-hand fingers, as in the second measure of the chorus. Keep the Bm chord fretted, and simply move your ring finger up to the 4th fret of the 5th string on beat 4 to get the C♯ bass note.

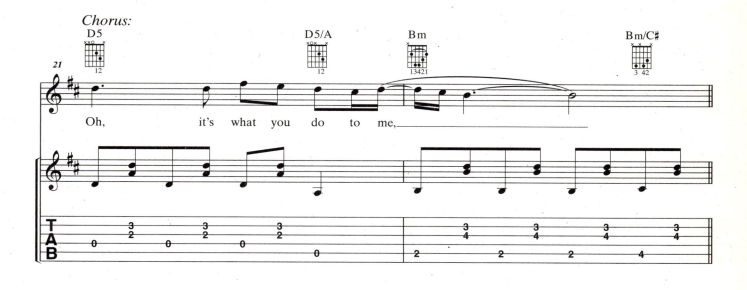

FUN FACT

The Delilah in "Hey There Delilah" is real, but the truth isn't exactly like the fairy-tale romance painted in the song. Long-distance runner Delilah DiCrescenzo met Tom Higgenson through a mutual friend in 2003, and Higgenson was so smitten by her that he promised to write her a song. He followed through with his promise, writing a huge hit, but the two never became romantically involved. Delilah did accompany Higgenson to the 2008 Grammy Awards, however, after the song was nominated for both Song of the Year and Best Pop Performance by a Duo or Group with Vocal.

Hey There Delilah

Words and Music by
TOM HIGGENSON

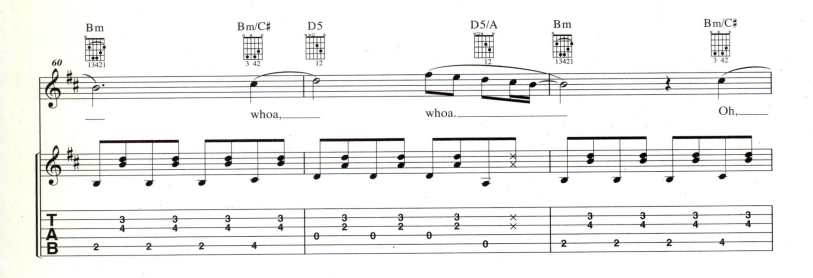

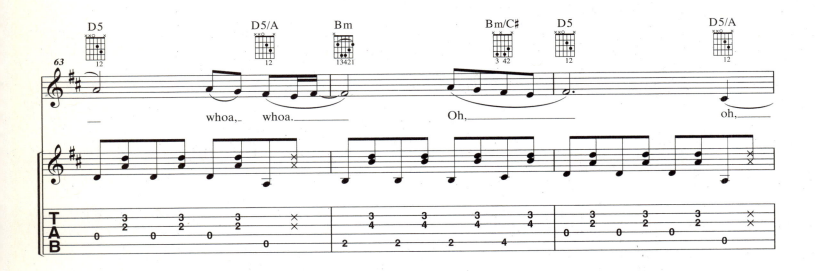

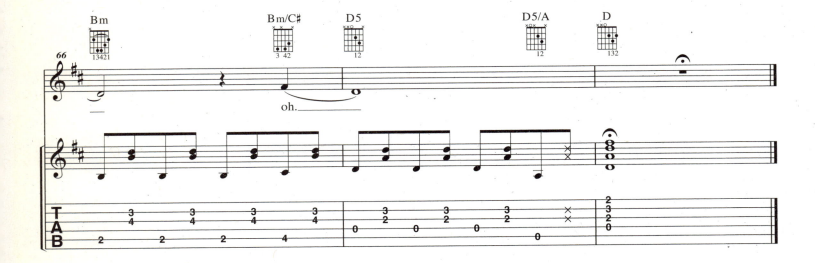

If You Could Read My Mind

Key Thoughts

Ontario-born Gordon Lightfoot performed on the folk circuit for over 10 years before becoming an "overnight" success in 1971 with the gentle ballad "If You Could Read My Mind."

Take Note

The guitar accompaniment for "If You Could Read My Mind" is a fairly simple fingerpicking pattern that repeats throughout the song. The thumb plays the bass note of each chord, which means it plays the 6th string for G, the 5th string for C, and the 4th string for D. The other fingers arpeggiate the chords and should remain fixed to their assigned strings: the index finger plays the 4th string, the middle finger plays the 3rd string, and the ring finger plays the 2nd string. (For more on the italic letters [*pima*] in the example below, see the lesson for "Babe I'm Gonna Leave You" on page 16.)

GUITAR GODS

GORDON LIGHTFOOT's 1970 single "If You Could Read My Mind," from the poor-selling album *Sit Down Young Stranger*, became such a big hit that his record company decided to capitalize on the success and in 1971 renamed the album *If You Could Read My Mind*. The record featured guitarist Red Shea and bassist Rick Haynes, who were Gordon's usual backing musicians of the time, but he also received help from some of the best on the Warner/Reprise label. The all-star band included Ry Cooder (bottleneck guitar and mandolin), John Sebastian (autoharp, harmonica, and electric guitar), and Van Dyke Parks (harmonium). Randy Newman even worked on string arrangements for two tracks. Throughout the 1970s, Lightfoot released one classic after another. His 1974 album *Sundown*, with its hit title track, went to No. 1 on the U.S. charts. Other hits of the era include "Carefree Highway," "The Circle Is Small," and "The Wreck of the Edmund Fitzgerald," which was an unexpected hit given that its lyrics were taken directly from a *Newsweek* article about the sinking of a ship during a severe storm. Despite the decline in popularity of folk music over the time of his lengthy career, Gordon Lightfoot continues to record and in 2004 released his 20th album, *Harmony*.

If You Could Read My Mind

Words and Music by
GORDON LIGHTFOOT

Capo 2nd fret to match recording.

Moderately ♩ = 122

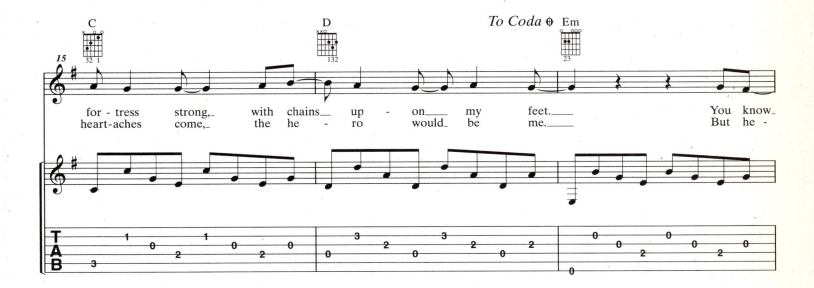

long as   I'm___   a ghost___   that you can't   see.___
cause the   end - ing's just___   too hard to   take._

Cont. rhy. simile

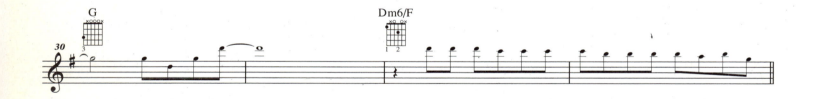

Bridge:

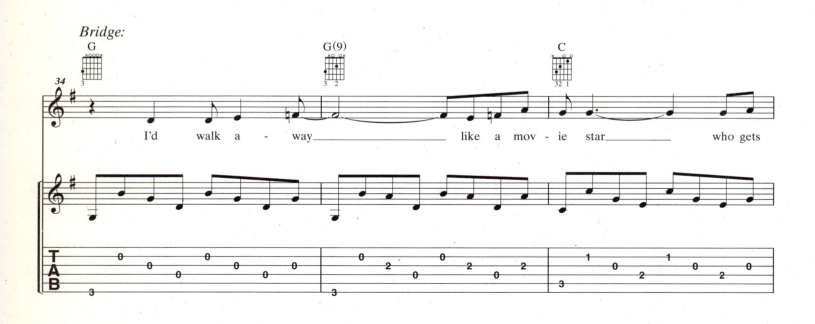

I'd   walk a - way_____   like a mov - ie star_____   who gets

Life by the Drop

Key Thoughts

After Stevie Ray Vaughan's tragic death in a helicopter accident, 10 tracks that were left off his previous records were posthumously released as *The Sky Is Crying*. Far better than an "outtakes" record, *The Sky Is Crying* is one of Vaughan's best albums, winning two Grammys (Best Contemporary Blues Album and Best Rock Instrumental Performance for "Little Wing"). "Life by the Drop" was the final track on *The Sky Is Crying*, and it features Stevie Ray Vaughan in a stripped-down setting—just his voice and an acoustic 12-string guitar.

Take Note

Stevie Ray Vaughan starts "Life by the Drop" with a few licks based on the A blues scale. The blues scale has six notes and is essentially a five-note minor pentatonic scale with the added ♭5. The A blues scale that Vaughan uses is notated below.

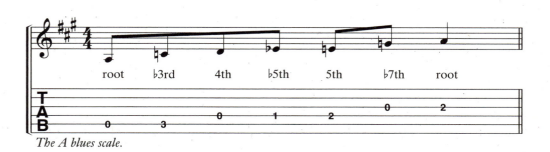

The A blues scale.

If you look through the first measures of the song, you'll see that Vaughan uses only these notes in the scale, with one exception—the D♯ in measure 1. But D♯ and E♭ are actually the same pitch; they're *enharmonic* notes.

DEFINITION

Enharmonic notes have the same pitch, but different names. For example, in "Life by the Drop," the D♯ in measure 1 and the E♭ in measure 2 are actually the exact same notes.

For the rhythm part, Vaughan plays a popular blues backup pattern that adds the 6th on beats 2 and 4 over the A, E, and D chords. Since Vaughan only plays the bottom two notes of each chord, you could opt to fret only those notes. If you finger the complete chords, you'll need to reach over with your pinky finger to grab those notes on the 4th fret. To do this, try using your index finger on the 2nd fret of the 4th string for the A chord, the 5th string for the E chord, and the 3rd string for the D chord. Then, just reach up with your ring finger to fret the 4th fret on beats 2 and 4 for whatever chord you're playing.

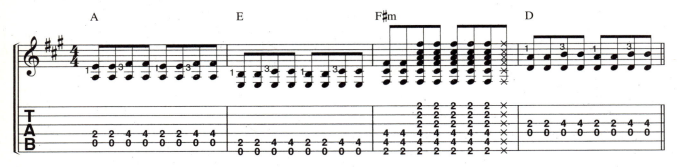

"Life by the Drop" is a blues *shuffle*, which means the basic quarter note pulse is sub-divided into triplet groups of three, not groups of two even eighth notes. The shuffle feel is also called *triplet feel*, and means that every pair of eighth notes should sound as if you're playing the first and third notes of an eighth-note triplet.

Written like this: **Sounds like this:**

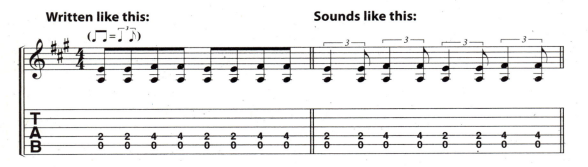

TIP

If you look to the right of the song's tempo, you'll see a rhythmic figure in parentheses that calls for the triplet feel. The triplet feel is often called a *shuffle feel* in blues and rock and *swing feel* in jazz. In swing, the triplet feel also incorporates a walking bass line, which is not found in a blues shuffle.

GUITAR GODS

STEVIE RAY VAUGHAN sounds great on an acoustic guitar, but it was his electric guitar prowess that earned him a place among his blues heroes. After cutting his teeth in Austin, Texas, with a variety of bands in the 1970s, Vaughan hooked up with the backing band Double Trouble in 1978. The ensemble's big break came when their set at the 1982 Montreaux Jazz Festival was noticed by David Bowie and Jackson Browne. Bowie asked Vaughan to play on his upcoming album, *Let's Dance*, and Browne offered Vaughan and Double Trouble free studio time. Bowie's record exposed Vaughan to an international audience, and Browne's generosity allowed the band to release their first of many records—*Texas Flood*.

Life by the Drop

Moderately ♩ = 97 (♫ = ♪³♪)

Words and Music by
DOYLE BRAMHALL and BARBARA LOGAN

*Acous. Gtr. simile on repeats.

* 3rd time only.   ** 2nd and 3rd times only.

Verse 2:
Up and down that road in our worn-out shoes,
Talkin' 'bout good things and singin' the blues.
You went your way and I stayed behind,
We both knew it was just a matter of time.

Livin' our dreams, oh, you on top,
My mind is achin', lord, it won't stop.
That's how it happens, livin' life by the drop.

Verse 3:
No wasted time, we're alive today,
Churnin' up the past, there's no easier way.
Times been between us, a means to an end,
God, it's good to be here walkin' together, my friend.

Livin' a dream...
My mind's stopped achin'...
That's how it happened livin' life by the drop.
That's how it happened livin' life by the drop.
That's how it happened livin' life by the drop.

How Can You Mend
a Broken Heart

Key Thoughts

Most popular artists are lucky to have just one long-running career, but the Bee Gees managed to carve out *two* distinctly different careers over their musical lifetime. Their first musical identity was characterized by a soft rock sound and ran from the late '60s through the early '70s; their second one featured a disco sound with soaring falsetto vocals and ran from the late '70s to the present. In the former category, "How Can You Mend a Broken Heart" was released in 1971 on the Bee Gees' album *Trafalgar*.

Take Note

If you listen to the version of "How Can You Mend a Broken Heart" we included on the CD, you'll notice that a triplet feel is used, resulting in the song's loping sound. You'll see this indicated at the beginning of the music as a rhythmic notation of two eighth notes equaling a bracketed quarter–eighth triplet. This means to play every pair of eighth notes as if they were eighth-note triplets with the first note being held for *two* notes of the triplet. (Just think "long–short.") As discussed in the previous lesson, this might be easier to feel and visualize by looking at how a triplet feel sounds (seen in the first example below). In the second example, you'll see the way this pattern looks when the triplet feel is implied and marked at the beginning of a song.

How a triplet feel sounds:

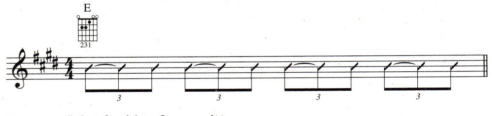

How a triplet feel is often written:

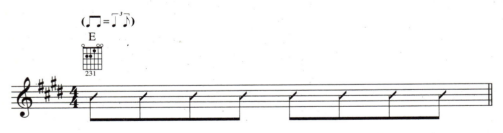

Once you have this triplet-feel strum pattern down, things will come together, since this strum pattern continues throughout the whole song. The difficult part, then, is to finger all the barre chords and the complicated-looking open-string chords found throughout. Don't let the names of those open-string chords throw you off; the open-string chords are—as you might suspect—the ones using open strings with shapes up the fretboard. If you have trouble sliding all the way up to the 6th fret for the Emaj7 chord, you can play an alternate version down at the nut, like this:

Emaj7

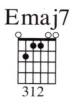

If you have trouble with barre chords, you can always use alternate shapes or partial chords. Here are some shapes you can try out as alternates for each barre chord, but feel free to use others if you're more comfortable with them.

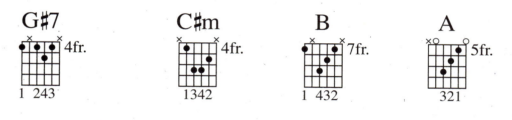

FUN FACT

The Bee Gees initially wrote "How Can You Mend a Broken Heart" for Andy Williams. He apparently passed, so the Bee Gees recorded the song themselves, and it became a No. 1 hit. (Williams, presumably, realized he made a mistake and later recorded the song.) Al Green included the hit on his 1972 release *Let's Stay Together*, and it's been covered by a host of other artists, including Barry Manilow and *American Idol* champion Ruben Studdard.

How Can You Mend
a Broken Heart

Into the Mystic

Key Thoughts

Van Morrison managed to follow up one of the most critically acclaimed albums of all time (*Astral Weeks*) with an equally heralded record: *Moondance*. The latter features at least *five* classic tunes, including the ethereal love song "Into the Mystic."

Take Note

Morrison played "Into the Mystic" in C position with a capo on the 3rd fret, propelling the track by using *scratch rhythm*. To play scratch rhythm, lift your left-hand fingers off the chord just enough to dampen the strings, then strum through with your picking hand. Dampen any open strings by adding other fingers or by rolling fingers over from fretted notes to cover those strings. Indicated by "x" noteheads in notation and TAB, scratch rhythm should sound like a percussive "chukka." If you hear any notes, you're not dampening the strings enough. If your fingers inadvertently sound harmonics, use more fingers or slide them over to a place on the string that doesn't create those harmonics.

In the example below (taken from measure 2), Morrison uses scratch rhythm on beat 2—which is a *backbeat*. Be sure to pay close attention to the voice moving from a 4th string open D to 2nd fret E that starts and ends the pattern.

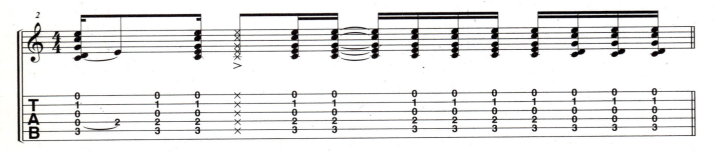

DEFINITION

In $\frac{4}{4}$ time, the **backbeats** are the weaker two beats in the measure. However, in most types of rock and pop music, the backbeat is accented, providing a strong feeling of forward momentum. Imagine a drummer playing the bass drum on beats 1 and 3—those are the strong beats. The drummer then usually strikes the snare, with a strong accent, on beats 2 and 4—the backbeats.

Throughout the verse and chorus, a nylon-string guitar adds fills up the neck, most of which are created by modifying a C shape to make Csus and Csus2 chords. If you use the finger-ings shown below, the hammer-on and pull-off lines in measures 3–5 will fall easily under your fingers:

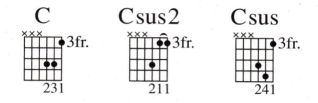

The nylon-string guitar creates other fills throughout the song (especially in the pre-chorus) by sliding 6th shapes on the 1st and 3rd strings (for more on 6th intervals, see Appendix A: Chord Theory). Notice how two different 6th patterns are used over each chord:

Sliding 6th Shapes

 TIP

To add extra drive to scratch rhythm on the backbeats, try slapping the middle strings with the palm of your picking hand at exactly the same time that your pick connects with the lower strings. This should add a little more punch, emulating a snare drum for solo guitar performances.

 FUN FACT

Van Morrison's given name was George Ivan Morrison, but he shortened his middle name to "Van," and the iconic moniker was born.

Into the Mystic

Words and Music by
VAN MORRISON

Capo 3rd fret to match recording.

Moderately slow ♩ = 84

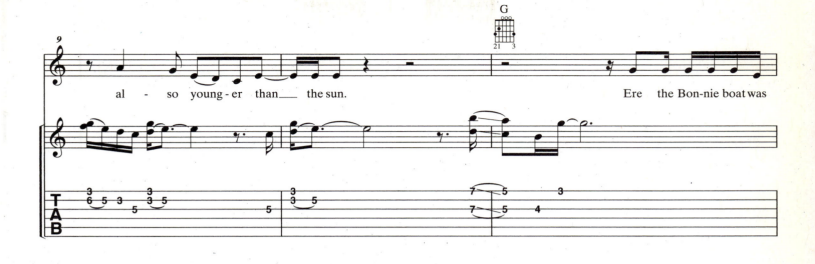

al - so young - er than___ the sun.   Ere the Bon-nie boat was

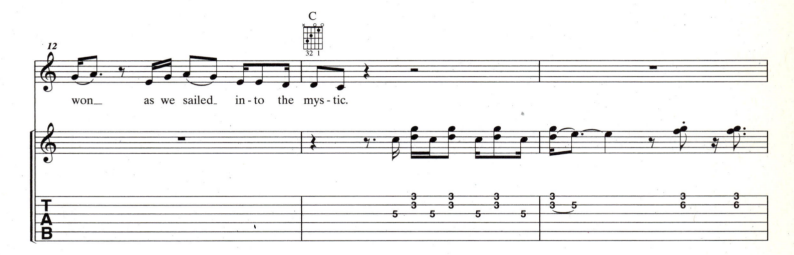

won___   as we sailed___ in - to   the mys - tic.

Acous. Gtr. 2 cont. simile

Hark   now,   I   hear   the   sail - ors   cry,___   smell   the   sea___   and___

feel the sky.___   Let your soul   and   spir-its fly_____ in-to the mys - tic.___

Layla
(*Unplugged* version)

Key Thoughts

In 1992, Eric Clapton appeared to completely reinvent his signature song "Layla" for his *MTV Unplugged* special. Performed on acoustic guitars with a lazy shuffle feel and without the original driving signature riff, this version was so different from the original that Clapton told the audience, "See if you can spot this one." The truth is, Clapton originally conceived the song in 1970 as a slow blues shuffle exactly as performed on the show. But after he had presented it to Duane Allman and his bandmates for a Derek & the Dominos recording session, Duane suggested they turn it into an up-tempo rocker, adding the now-famous opening riff used in the electric version.

Take Note

The song has an underlying *shuffle* feel, meaning that the eighth notes are played long-short instead of exactly even. Listen carefully to the provided recording and imitate the feel.

The main acoustic guitar part is a two-bar pattern. It's right up front in the intro, repeated on each chorus, and can be played throughout the guitar solo section. Follow the left hand fingerings as shown below in the notation and chord frames.

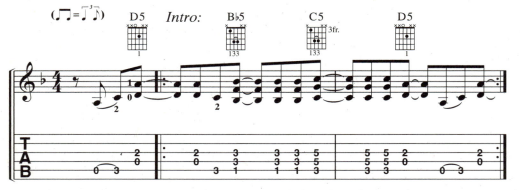

If you want to try improvising a guitar solo, work with the D minor pentatonic scale as shown in the figure below, which spans three positions on the neck of the guitar. Try improvising melodies both vertically (across the strings) and horizontally (up and down single strings).

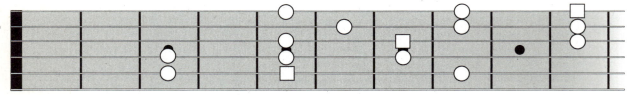

The D minor pentatonic scale:

GUITAR GODS

Though internationally revered as one of the greatest guitarists of his generation, **ERIC CLAPTON** was surprisingly reluctant to break out as a solo artist. In 1970, his self-titled solo debut album peaked at No. 13, but before the record even hit store shelves, he'd taken himself out of the spotlight to form Derek & the Dominos. Four years and a kicked drug addiction later, Clapton made his permanent return as a solo artist with *461 Ocean Boulevard*, reaching No. 1.

Layla
(*Unplugged* version)

Words and Music by
ERIC CLAPTON and JIM GORDON

Moderately ♩ = 96

Intro:

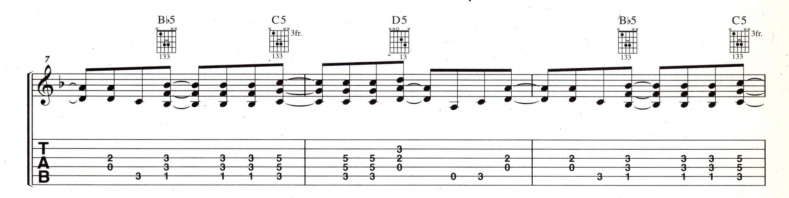

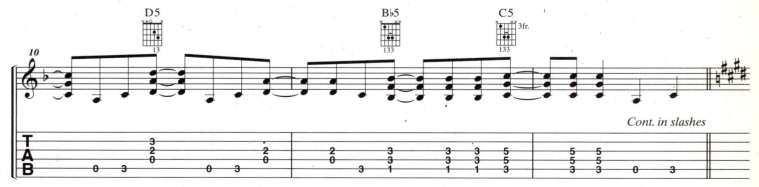

Cont. in slashes

Margaritaville

Key Thoughts

"Margaritaville" isn't a set of coordinates on a map; it's a state of mind. Jimmy Buffett and his legions of "Parrotheads" (the fans who've adopted his music and his message) live there, on the beach, basking in the sun.

Take Note

This is a classic three-chord song. The only chords you need to know to play this song are D, G, and A. In the music, you will see a few variations on these three chords, like Dsus and A7. Add those only if you can play the basic D and A with total confidence.

This is a strumming song. Hold your pick loosely (but don't drop it!), and swing your wrist in a very steady up-and-down motion, which should be in perfect timing to the up-and-down tapping of your foot. Don't strike the strings on every strum or it will sound too busy. Instead, play on most of the down-strums and some of the up-strums. Find a rhythm that works for you, one that makes it easy for you to sing the song. The diagram below is just one suggestion for a simple strum pattern.

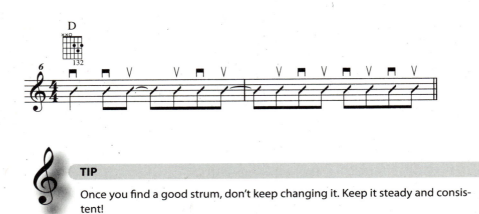

TIP

Once you find a good strum, don't keep changing it. Keep it steady and consistent!

The four-measure introduction is the signature guitar part of this song. By the time you've played the first few beats, everyone will know you're in "Margaritaville." To play the pattern, lock your 1st finger down on the 1st string (the high E), and practice playing just the notes on the 1st string. Follow the TAB, and use the provided sound-alike and play-along recordings to guide you in playing the correct rhythm. Once you can play the melody on the 1st string with one finger, place your 3rd finger down on the 2nd string, lock your 1st and 3rd fingers into this position, and again use your 1st finger to guide this two-finger "grip" as shown in the TAB. All the notes that are two frets apart are played with a 1st- and 3rd-finger grip. In the third measure, use a 1st- and 2nd-finger grip to play the notes that are one fret apart (7–8 and 2–3). Your 1st finger should never leave the 1st string.

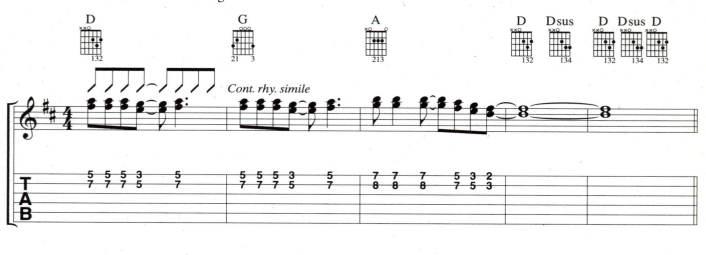

FUN FACT

Since Jimmy Buffett is friends with legendary investment guru and billionaire Warren Buffett, there's been much speculation that the two very successful men are related. Even the famous Buffetts themselves wondered, and they took a DNA test in 2007 to get the truth. In the end, no close blood relation was found.

Margaritaville

Words and Music by
JIMMY BUFFETT

D.S. 𝄉 al Coda

Coda

Cont. rhy. simile

Yes, and some_ peo - ple claim__ that there's_ a

wom - an to blame_____ and I know__ it's my own_ damn_ fault._

Verse 2:
Don't know the reason,
I stayed here all season
With nothing to show but this brand-new tattoo.
But it's a real beauty,
A Mexican cutie,
How it got here I haven't a clue.
(To Chorus:)

Verse 4:
I blew out my flip-flop,
Stepped on a pop-top;
Cut my heel, had to cruise on back home.
But there's booze in the blender,
And soon it will render
That frozen concoction that helps me hang on.
(To Chorus:)

Verse 3:*
Old men in tank tops
Cruising the gift shops
Checking out the chiquitas down by the shore.
They dream about weight loss,
Wish they could be their own boss.
Those three-day vacations become such a bore.

*"Lost" verse (Live version only)

Moondance

Key Thoughts

The title track from Van Morrison's February 1970 album, "Moondance" has become a staple of classic-rock radio. Curiously, the song wasn't an instant success, though a large part of this may be because it wasn't initially released as a single. It's a testament to the song's power that it still managed to find its way onto the Billboard Hot 100 chart—seven years later!

Take Note

Van Morrison provides a rhythm foundation in the verses by strumming a repeated Am–Bm(4)/A–Am7–Bm(4)/A chord progression. Don't let the complicated-looking Bm(4)/A *slash chord* intimidate you; it's just the Am chord shape slid up two frets, played with the two open strings from the Am chord. For the Am7 shape, barre your ring finger across strings 2–4, adding the open A string underneath.

DEFINITION

Slash chords have a note other than the root (the letter after which a chord is named) in the bass. These chords are labeled with the chord name followed by a slash with and bass note. Sometimes the bass note is a chord tone, and sometimes it isn't.

At the chorus, Morrison plays some *syncopated* chord stabs using barre chords up the neck. To *syncopate* means to accent the weak beats. Notice how Morrison does this by playing heavy strums on the eighth note before the strongest beats of each measure (beats 1 and 3). If you find playing barre chord shapes like these difficult, you can always substitute root-position versions of these chords, like the ones below.

Am

231

Dm

231

Pay close attention to the quarter-note triplets just before the chorus and in the final line of the song. Quarter-note triplets fit three equal notes into the space of two quarter notes, and they can be a difficult rhythm to feel. Play along with the included recording to get the hang of this. The TNT software will make it easier if you slow things down until you feel the rhythm internally, then speed the song up to performance tempo. At the end of the song, you can avoid barre chords by using the Am and Dm chord shapes on the previous page along with these root-position forms:

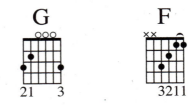

FUN FACT

Cover versions of "Moondance" have been recorded by literally *hundreds* of acts. The universal appeal of this song lends itself to a diversity of styles, and you'll find recorded vocal and instrumental versions from a wide range of artists such as Greg Brown, Sun Ra, Michael Bublé, Nana Mouskouri, Bobby McFerrin, Andreas Vollenweider, Kathie Lee Gifford, and countless others.

Moondance

Words and Music by
VAN MORRISON

Maggie May

Key Thoughts

Prior to "Maggie May," raspy-voiced Rod Stewart had enjoyed some success as both the vocalist for the Jeff Beck Group and frontman for the band Faces. But it was this inadvertent chart-topper that really launched Rod's solo career in 1971. The song was originally released as the B-side to Rod Stewart's "Reason to Believe" single. When British DJs began playing the flip side instead of the intended A-side, "Maggie May" began its ascendancy to rock classic status.

Co-written by Stewart and Martin Quittenton, the lyrics are a largely autobiographical tale of a young man's sexual relationship with an older woman.

"Maggie May" has the distinction of being one of the first rock songs to feature a mandolin, making it an unwitting precursor to Led Zeppelin's "The Battle of Evermore." The mandolin on the record was played by British folk-rock musician Ray Jackson.

Take Note

The acoustic on the original recording is a 12-string guitar and, though not essential, it is really helpful to hear the octave notes of a 12-string in the song's intro. While picking out the indicated notes of each arpeggio, hold your fingers down in the chord shape and allow the notes to ring throughout. Be sure the open 3rd string sustains while you play the little embellishments on the G chord in measures 3 and 7.

For the acoustic guitar, the verse and guitar solo sections are a simple exercise in strumming open-position chords. Have fun!

The first electric guitar solo is transcribed in this arrangement. It is perfectly possible to play this solo on an acoustic guitar. If the bends prove too difficult, you can substitute them with slides (up one fret for a half step, up two frets for a full step). This solo is a great example of tasteful use of the D major pentatonic scale.

D major (B minor) pentatonic scale.

The mandolin part in the coda would also probably sound better on a 12-string guitar (if you have one), because both mandolins and 12-strings have a pair of strings for each note. If you don't have a 12-string, don't worry. Also, if it's not possible to play all the way up at the 17th fret on your guitar, transpose the notes down an octave by subtracting 12 from each of the TAB numbers. For example, a note on the 15th fret of the 1st string is an octave lower on the 3rd fret of the 1st string (15–12=3). Use alternate picking (down- and up-strokes) on the sixteenth notes.

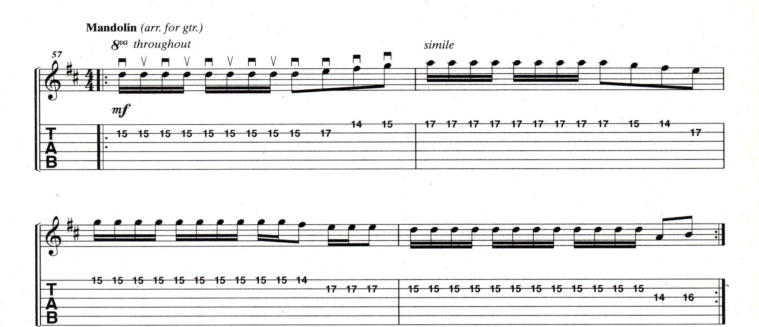

GUITAR GODS

The guitarist on this track, **RON WOOD**, was Rod Stewart's bandmate in both the Jeff Beck Group and Faces. Within four years, Ron received an invitation to join "The World's Greatest Rock 'n' Roll Band"—The Rolling Stones. Thirty-five years later, Woody is still rolling with Mick, Keith, and Charlie, though he still occasionally jams with his old buddy Rod.

Maggie May

Words and Music by
ROD STEWART and MARTIN QUITTENTON

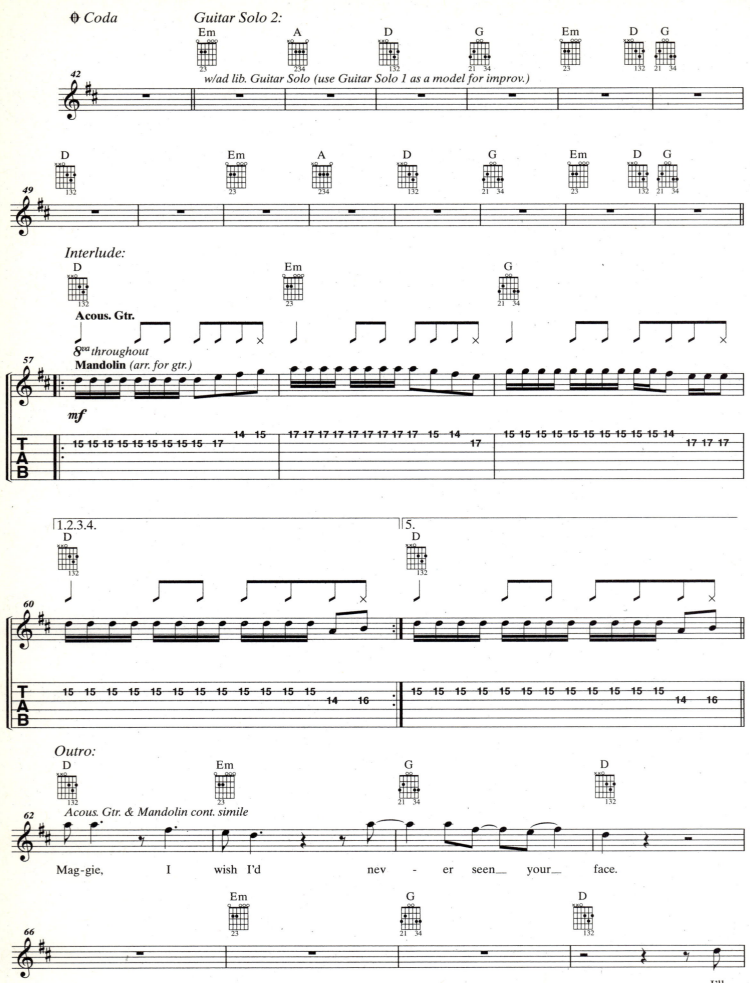

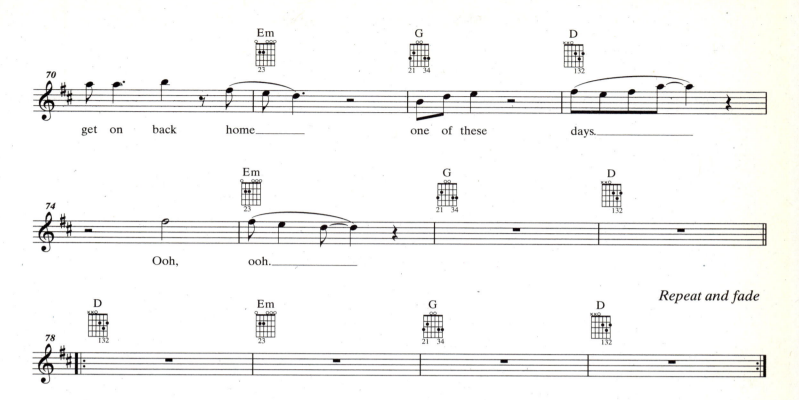

get on back home_____   one of these   days._____

Ooh,   ooh._____

Repeat and fade

Verse 2:
The morning sun, when it's in your face,
Really shows your age.
But that don't worry me none,
In my eyes you're everything.
I laughed at all of your jokes,
My love you didn't need to coax.
Oh, Maggie, I couldn't have tried anymore.
You lead me away from home
Just to save you from being alone.
You stole my soul and that's a
Pain I can do without.

Verse 3:
All I needed was a friend
To lend a guiding hand.
But you turned into a lover and, mother,
What a lover, you wore me out.
All you did was wreck my bed,
And in the morning kick me in the head.
Oh, Maggie, I couldn't have tried anymore.
You lead me away from home
'Cause you didn't want to be alone.
You stole my heart,
I couldn't leave you if I tried.
(To Guitar Solo 1:)

Verse 4:
I suppose I could collect my books
And get on back to school.
Or steal my daddy's cue,
And make a living out of playing pool.
Or find myself a rock and roll band
That needs a helping hand.
Oh, Maggie, I wish I'd never seen your face.
You made a first-class fool out of me,
But I'm as blind as a fool can be.
You stole my heart
But I love you anyway.
(To Guitar Solo 2:)

Melissa

Key Thoughts

The album *Eat a Peach* was a turning point for The Allman Brothers Band, mostly because their fiery and influential guitarist, Duane Allman, died in a motorcycle accident midway through the recording sessions. By the time "Melissa" was penned and ready to record, Duane was no longer around, and sole guitarist Dickey Betts took over lead duties. Gregg Allman co-wrote "Melissa" with Steve Alaimo in 1968 and, while the bulk of the lyrics talk of a roving gypsy longing to return to his lover, the final verse's question, "Will you hide the dead man's ghost?" hints that Gregg may have been thinking about his brother when the song was finally recorded.

Take Note

Gregg starts the song with a great open-string chord pattern played as a three-note shape (the middle three notes of a barred minor-chord shape) that slides up the neck. Don't let the complicated names of the *slash chords* intimidate you; instead, just think about the shapes and sounds. (For more on slash chords, see the notes for "Moondance" on page 103.)

While Gregg strums his acoustic, Dickey Betts lays down licks on electric guitar. You can play these licks on an acoustic if you have a cutaway or, of course, use an electric guitar. Betts constructs most of these licks from an E major pentatonic scale (E–F♯–G♯–B–C♯) that spans two positions:

The E major pentatonic scale.

It's easy to shift to the higher position when you slide your ring finger along the 3rd string from the 11th fret up to the 13th fret (the same move works well on the way down the scale). Betts does deviate slightly from this pattern, most notably by adding extra notes—all taken from the E major scale (E–F♯–G♯–A–B–C♯–D♯).

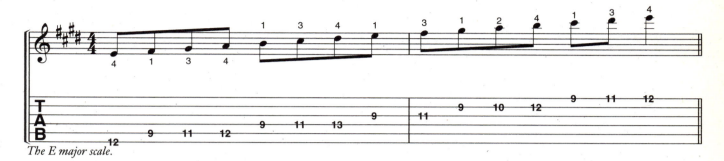

The E major scale.

If you have trouble holding the long bends for their full value, make sure to reinforce them with your other fingers. For example, on the whole-step bend at the end of the chorus (measures 17–18), bend with your ring finger, but back it up with *both* your index and middle fingers.

TIP

If you want to play the electric leads on your acoustic, you'll certainly need a cutaway to get up to the 17th fret. But you'll also find that stringing your guitar with light or extra light strings will allow you to bend more easily. If you want to bend the 3rd string, it often helps to replace it with an unwound string.

GUITAR GODS

DUANE ALLMAN was one of the most influential guitarists of the 20th century. Though his life and career were too short, he managed to produce a slew of studio and live Allman Brothers Band recordings, as well as a wealth of material backing others. As the session guitarist for the Muscle Shoals Sound Studio, Duane played on famous recordings by quite a few artists, including songs by Wilson Pickett, Aretha Franklin, and Boz Scaggs. Perhaps even more notably, he dueled with Eric Clapton on Derek and the Dominos' album *Layla and Other Assorted Love Songs*, playing some of the record's most recognizable licks and solos, such as the opening lick and closing slide solo of "Layla." Of course, Dickey Betts is quite an accomplished guitarist, too. In addition to the beautiful lines he played on "Melissa," Dickey has had many exceptional live solos and duet leads with Duane and the more recent Allman Brothers Band guitarists, Warren Haynes and Derek Trucks.

Melissa

Words and Music by
STEVE ALAIMO and
GREGG ALLMAN

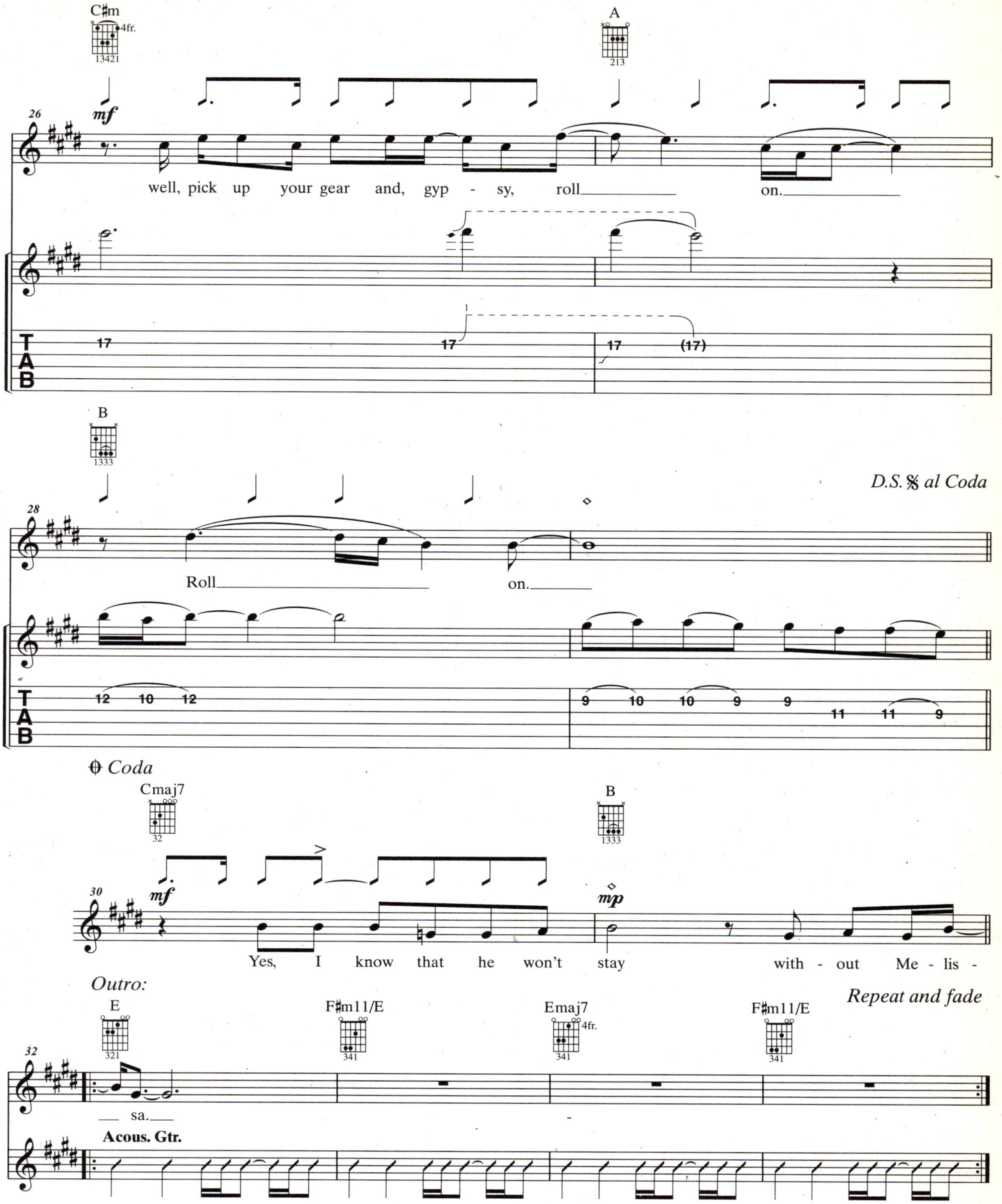
C♯m
A
mf
well, pick up your gear and, gyp - sy, roll on.
B
D.S. 𝄋 al Coda
Roll on.
⊕ Coda
Cmaj7
B
mf
mp
Yes, I know that he won't stay with - out Me - lis -
Outro:
E
F♯m11/E
Emaj7
F♯m11/E
Repeat and fade
sa.
Acous. Gtr.

Verse 2:
Freight train, each car looks the same, all the same.
And no one knows the gypsy's name,
No one hears his lonely sigh.
There are no blankets where he lies.
In all his deepest dreams, the gypsy flies
With sweet Melissa.

Verse 3:
Crossroads, will you ever let him go? (Lord, Lord).
Will you hide the dead man's ghost?
Or will he lie beneath the clay?
Or will his spirit float away?
But I know that he won't stay
Without Melissa.
(To Coda)

She Talks to Angels

Key Thoughts

The Black Crowes appeared on the national scene in 1990 with their debut record, *Shake Your Moneymaker*. The band's pitch-perfect recreation of classic rock in The Rolling Stones' vein immediately connected with music fans who were tired of hair bands and synthesized sounds. One of two hot singles on the record, "She Talks to Angels," helped establish The Black Crowes as the classic-rock band of the '90s.

Take Note

Guitarist Rich Robinson tunes his acoustic guitar to an *altered tuning* to play "She Talks to Angels." Specifically, he's in an *open tuning* (Open E). (For more on altered and open tunings, see the lesson for "Big Yellow Taxi" on page 32.)

To get into Open E tuning, you'll need to tune your 4th and 5th strings up a whole step to E and B, respectively, and your 3rd string up a half step to G♯. If you don't have a tuner to check yourself, start by tuning your 5th string to match the 7th fret of your 6th string; then tune your 4th string to match the 5th fret of your 5th string; finally, tune the 3rd string to match the 4th fret of your 4th string. Make sure to tune the strings in this order, since some of the strings you're using as reference points need to be tuned *before* they're used to check the next string. In case that's not clear, here's a diagram to show how you can do this:

Tuning up to Open E tuning

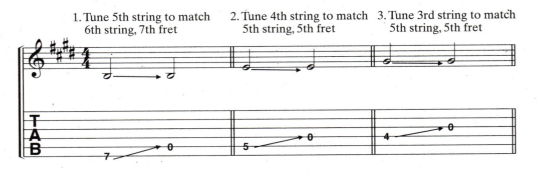

1. Tune 5th string to match 6th string, 7th fret
2. Tune 4th string to match 5th string, 5th fret
3. Tune 3rd string to match 5th string, 5th fret

Tuning your guitar up to Open E places a lot of tension on the strings. You might even break a string. So instead of tuning up, many guitarists tune down to Open D—the exact same tuning as Open E, but down a whole step. Then you can just place a capo at the 2nd fret to match the key of the recording.

Open D: D–A–D–F♯–A–D

As you play through the song, pay close attention to the TAB numbers and chord frames, since notes on the 3rd, 4th, and 5th strings won't sound the way you might expect. Strum using a sixteenth-note strum pattern, using down-strokes for every eighth-note subdivision, and up-strokes for any sixteenth notes that fall between. If you count "1–ee–&–ah, 2–ee–&–ah," you'll be playing down-strokes on "1" and "&" and "2" and "&." This means you'll play up-strokes on the "ee" and "ah" sixteenth notes that fall between, as shown below.

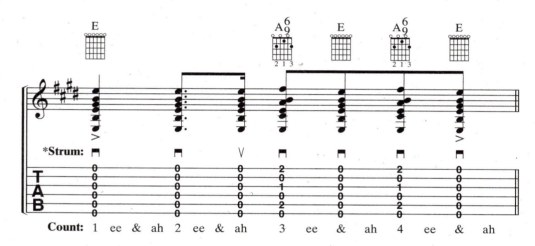

Watch out for the *harmonics* that show up throughout the song. If you haven't played harmonics before, see the tip below.

DEFINITION

Harmonics are high-ringing bell-like overtones that sound when you pluck a string while touching it lightly with your fretting hand.

TIP

In the transcription, you'll see harmonics notated by diamond-headed notes along with the abbreviation "harm." placed between notation and TAB staves. To sound these notes, place your fret-hand finger *directly* over the fretwire, lightly touch the string while you pluck it, then immediately lift your fret-hand finger off the string. This technique takes a while to master, but if you're patient, you'll eventually get it.

She Talks to Angels

Gtr. tuned in Open E:

⑥ = E   ③ = G#
⑤ = B   ② = B
④ = E   ① = E

Words and Music by
CHRIS ROBINSON and RICH ROBINSON

Slow ballad ♩ = 80

Intro:

*A6/9 chord occurs as an embellishment on every occurance of Rhy. Fig. 1.

D.S. 𝄋 al Coda

Verse 3:
She keeps a lock of hair in her pocket.
She wears a cross around her neck.
The hair is from a little boy,
And the cross from someone she has not met.
Well, not yet.
(To Chorus:)

Verse 4:
Repeat Verse 2

Sister Golden Hair

Key Thoughts

"Sister Golden Hair" topped the Billboard Hot 100 chart in 1975; it was the band America's second No. 1 single, after "A Horse with No Name." Released on their fifth album, *Hearts*, "Sister Golden Hair" was penned by Gerry Beckley. It was common in the band for the person who wrote the song to sing it, and this was the case with "Sister Golden Hair"—Beckley sang the lead vocal while the band's other singer-songwriters (Dewey Bunnell and Dan Peek) backed him up with harmonies.

Take Note

Use the suggested strumming pattern to play acoustic guitar part. (Remember: V means up-stroke, and ⊓ means down-stroke.) As you can see, the pattern has consecutive down-strokes and up-strokes in some places. This may make you want to pause between strums, but pausing breaks the steady rhythm. Instead, keep your strumming arm moving up and down in a constant motion often called *pendulum strumming*. Connect with the strings for every down- or up-stroke indicated, and strum through the air whenever a strum isn't indicated.

DEFINITION

Pendulum strumming gets its name from the way your arm moves when using this technique. Just as a pendulum constantly moves back and forth, your strumming arm constantly moves up and down. Simply keep your arm moving and strum through the air for any down- or up-strokes that you don't want to sound. This avoids breaks in the rhythm that can occur by pausing at the top or the bottom of a strum.

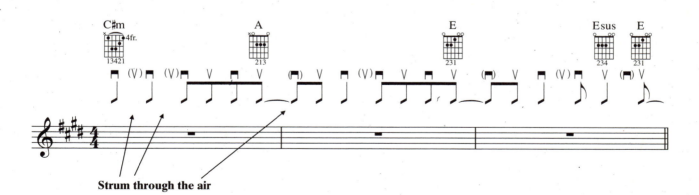

Strum through the air

For the electric slide part, try wearing the slide on your ring or pinky finger. This allows you to use your other fingers to mute strings that aren't being played. You may also want to mute the string that the slide *is* playing to dampen unwanted noise. When you do this, make sure to dampen the string *behind* the slide (closer to the nut of your guitar), since muting closer to the soundhole will completely dampen the string.

FUN FACT

"Sister Golden Hair" features an accidental lyric revision, courtesy of Jackson Browne. Browne toured with America, and he would sing songs with the band backstage. Beckley had originally written the line "Will you meet me in the middle, will you meet me in VA," but Browne mis-heard the abbreviation for "Virginia" (VA) as "the air," and sang it that way. Beckley liked it better and changed the lyric to "will you meet me in the air."

GUITAR GODS

Dewey Bunnell, Dan Peek, and Gerry Beckley were all sons of U.S. Air Force officers stationed in the U.K. in the late '60s. The three met in high school, formed **AMERICA** shortly thereafter, and were barely out of their teens when they tasted success with 1971's "A Horse with No Name."

Sister Golden Hair

Moderately fast ♩ = 137

Words and Music by
GERRY BECKLEY

Never Going Back Again

Key Thoughts

Lindsey Buckingham used this song to develop his *Travis picking* technique, which is named for country great Merle Travis. It is a fingerpicking technique in which the right hand thumb *never* stops playing quarter notes, constantly alternating between two strings. This technique can seem tricky at first, but once you get the hang of it, it's pretty easy. Your right hand begins to play the pattern automatically, and then you just have to change the left hand chords as needed.

Take Note

Before starting to play, you need to tune your low E string down a whole step to D. This is known as *Drop D tuning*, and is a very common variation on standard tuning. Next, if you want to match the key of the original recording, place a capo at the 4th fret.

Before attempting the Travis pattern, start by playing just the thumb pattern shown in the first example below. Keep playing it until your thumb goes on automatic. Try watching TV with a guitar in your lap and just play the pattern over and over.

The first measure of this pattern in the song uses a pinch technique. While your thumb continues to play on each quarter note, your middle finger plays a note at the same time on beats 2 and 4; you "pinch" the bass note and the top note between your thumb and finger. The second measure is more complicated. It requires playing notes in between thumb strokes. Practice the two-bar example below until your fingers can play it without your brain having to think about it. Always use your thumb *p* to play the alternating bass-line notes, your index finger *i* on the 3rd string, your middle finger *m* on the 2nd string, and your ring finger *a* on the 1st string.

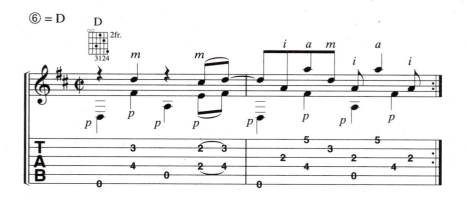

One of the most recognizable parts of this song is the way Lindsey gets a constant "rolling" pattern going, as in the two bars below. The A13(no 3rd) chord is a bit of a stretch. Hold the chord, get the alternating thumb pattern going, and then add the pinches and the in-between notes with your fingers.

GUITAR GODS

FLEETWOOD MAC actually started out as an English blues trio formed by guitar player Peter Green in the 1960s, but Green departed, Christine McVie joined, and the Fleetwood Mac we all came to know was formed in 1975 when the soft-rock duo of Stevie Nicks and Lindsey Buckingham joined the group. The new members helped turn the band into hit makers just at the point when the band was about to become a thing of the past. The quintet's second album was the blockbuster *Rumours*. Released in 1977, *Rumours* reached No. 1 and stayed there for 31 weeks. The record eventually sold over 17 million copies, making it one of the best-selling albums of all time.

The story of the making of *Rumours* is legendary. The album was recorded while every member of the band was going through a personal crisis: Mick Fleetwood divorced his wife right before the recording sessions, and both of the couples in the band (John and Christine McVie, and Buckingham and Nicks) were breaking up. Songs like "Go Your Own Way," "Never Going Back Again," "Dreams," and "You Make Loving Fun" (this last one written by Christine McVie about the man she was having an affair with) come off like journal entries. The term "confessional" music was probably never so appropriate, and the fact that the album was recorded at all is extraordinary. It is no wonder why *Rumours* continues to appeal to just about everyone, with its nearly universal themes served on a platter of easy-listening pop music.

Never Going Back Again

Gtr. 1 ⑥ = D and capo IV

Words and Music by
LINDSEY BUCKINGHAM

Moderately brisk in 2 ♩ = 88

Intro:

*Recording sounds a major 3rd higher than written.

1. She broke down__ and let me__ in,_____
2. You don't know what it means to__ win._____

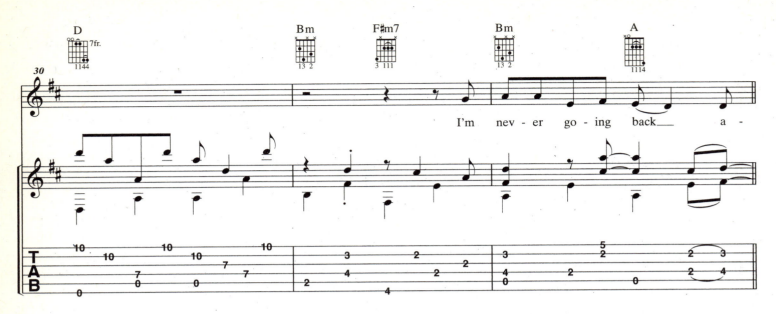

Peaceful Easy Feeling

Key Thoughts

The list of amazing hits from Eagles seems endless at times, but perhaps more than any other song, "Peaceful Easy Feeling" helped define their quintessential, Southern California sound. The song almost demands to be listened to in the car—top down, cruising the Pacific Coast Highway in Malibu.

Take Note

This is another classic strumming song—just a few basic chords, a simple strum pattern, and a little Malibu sunshine. For a good strum technique, hold the pick loosely between your thumb and index finger and swing your wrist in a constant down-up pattern. Strum all the strings of each chord on the down-stroke, but the up-stroke should only catch the top three strings. This happens pretty naturally if you are strumming from your wrist with a loose, arc-like motion.

The introduction is simply E to Esus as shown below. Use similar strumming patterns throughout the whole song.

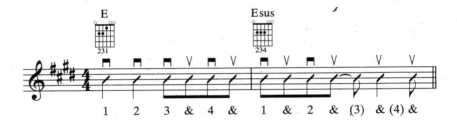

Whenever you move from one chord to the next, try to find a common note or some other way a finger can be used as a pivot point. This makes for smooth and easy chord changes, such as the move from E to A in the verse. In this case, the 1st finger can be used as a pivot point. From the E chord, slide your 1st finger up from the 1st fret to the 2nd fret and, as you slide, release your 2nd and 3rd fingers from the 4th and 5th strings and reposition them on the 4th and 2nd strings to form the A chord. Changing from A to E is simply the same process in reverse. Notice the accents on beats 2 and 4 of the constant eighth-note strum pattern as well. Play the accents as shown, and experiment with different patterns by sounding and muting chords on various beats.

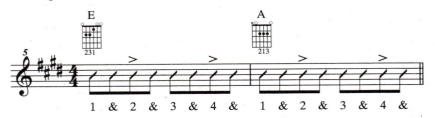

GUITAR GODS

Released in June 1972, **EAGLES'** self-titled debut introduced the world to Glenn Frey, Don Henley, Bernie Leadon, and Randy Meisner. *Eagles* made the Top 20 and eventually reached gold with the hits "Take It Easy," "Witchy Woman," and "Peaceful Easy Feeling." This rock and roll/country/folk-influenced LP is known for the nearly equal songwriting efforts from all members of the group, and even includes songs co-written by greats such as Jackson Browne ("Take It Easy"), Gene Clark ("Train Leaves Here This Morning"), and Jack Tempchin ("Peaceful Easy Feeling"). Several songs from this record are prominently featured on the best-selling record of all time, *Eagles: Their Greatest Hits 1971–1975.*

Peaceful Easy Feeling

Words and Music by
JACK TEMPCHIN

Verse 2:
And I found out a long time ago
What a woman can do to your soul.
Ah, but she can't take you anyway,
You don't already know how to go.
(To Chorus:)

Verse 3:
Instrumental

Verse 4:
I get this feelin' I may know you
As a lover and a friend.
But this voice keeps whispering in my other ear,
Tells me I may never see you again.
(To Chorus:)

Take It Easy

Key Thoughts

"Take It Easy" introduced Eagles to the world, and it remained a signature song throughout the band's long and successful career. The lead-off track to their 1972 self-titled debut record, "Take It Easy" was also released as a single and climbed to No. 12 on the Billboard Hot 100 chart. Sung by Glenn Frey, the song features lead guitar and banjo by Bernie Leadon.

Take Note

The acoustic guitar plays a driving strum pattern throughout the song. The "x" note-heads in the pattern represent partial chord strums (not dampened strings, which are also often notated with "x" noteheads). These strums most often happen in the transition between chords; while fret-hand fingers move to a new chord, the partial chord on open strings gets strummed. Here's how the first few measures of the acoustic guitar part look in notation and TAB, as well as slash notation:

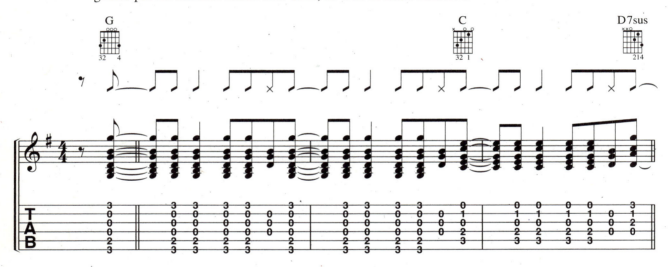

Notice the open-string (and partial chord) strums; in slash notation, these are "x"s. Strumming the open strings of partial chord shapes between chords isn't that noticeable, and it's a great trick for allowing more time to get your fingers into place for the next chord.

Guitarist Bernie Leadon plays lead guitar throughout, bending a lot of notes down near the nut, which is a tough place to bend due to string tension. Make sure to support the bending finger with another finger or two.

Leadon constructs a memorable solo by building melodic lines, staying mostly within the G major pentatonic scale. He starts in the root-position shape shown below, then later moves up the fretboard to higher versions of the scale:

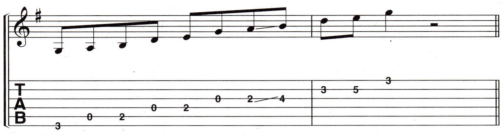

The G major pentatonic scale.

Also notice how he transfers the G lick in measure 42 up to D in measure 43 simply by moving it up the fretboard until it fits over a D chord. He repeats this lick in G again at measure 49—this time up an octave, and with a bend instead of a slide. Repeating ideas in this way helps make solos more memorable—a useful trick to use in your own playing.

FUN FACT

Jackson Browne co-wrote "Take It Easy" with Glenn Frey. It's reported that the two songwriters were neighbors at the time, and Frey had heard an early version of a tune that Browne was working on. Frey liked it so much that he added some lyrics and convinced Browne to let him use it with Eagles. Browne later released his own version on his second album, *For Everyman.*

GUITAR GODS

EAGLES were formed in 1971 by drummer Don Henley, bassist Randy Meisner, and guitarists Bernie Leadon and Glenn Frey. All band members were capable singers, allowing them to create the lush harmonies that became part of their signature sound. Multi-instrumentalist Bernie Leadon played lead guitar during the band's early years, and later incarnations of the band featured two other guitar heroes: Joe Walsh and Don Felder. The only other addition to the band was Timothy B. Schmit, who assumed bass duties after Randy Meisner quit.

Take It Easy

Words and Music by
JACKSON BROWNE
and GLENN FREY

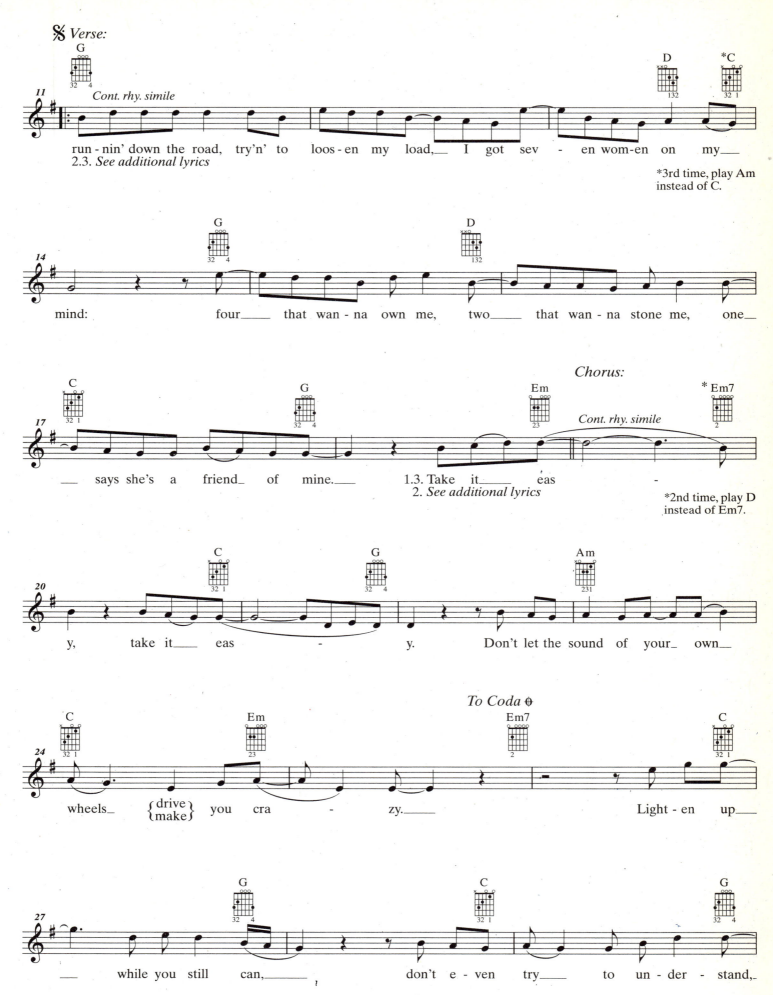

just find a place to make your stand, and take it eas -

y. Elec. Gtr.

2. Well, I'm a - y. Elec. Gtr.

Guitar Solo:

Acous. Gtr. cont. rhy. simile

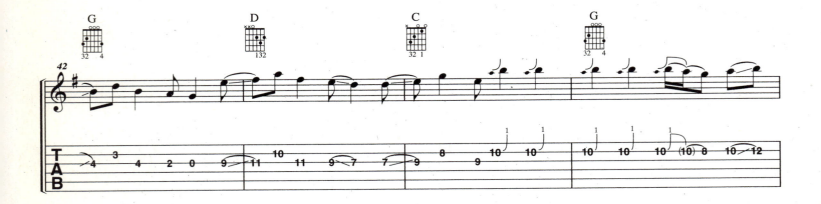

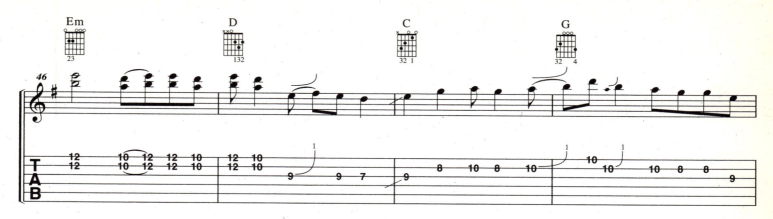

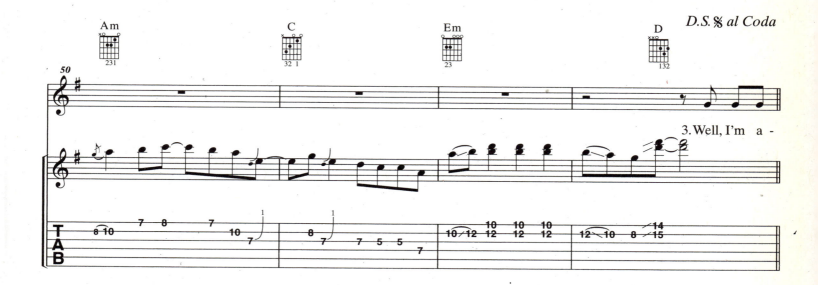

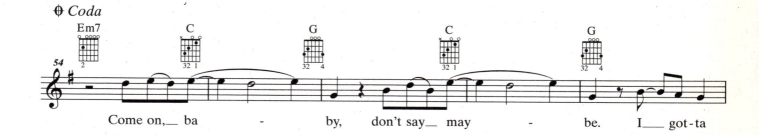

Come on,__ ba - by, don't say__ may - be. I__ got-ta

know if your__ sweet love__ is gon - na save_____ me.__

Outro:

Ooh,_____ ooh,_____ ooh,_____ ooh._____ Ooh,_____

ooh,_____ ooh,_____ ooh._____ Ooh,_____ Oh,_ we got it
(Ooh._____)

eas - y. We ought-ta take it

eas - y.

Verse 2:
Well, I'm a-standin' on a corner in Winslow, Arizona,
And such a fine sight to see:
It's a girl, my Lord, in a flatbed Ford
Slowin' down to take a look at me.

Chorus 2:
Come on, baby, don't say maybe.
I gotta know if your sweet love is gonna save me.
We may lose and we may win,
Though we will never be here again.
So open up, I'm climbin' in, so take it easy.
(To Guitar Solo:)

Verse 3:
Well, I'm a-runnin' down the road, tryin' to loosen my load,
Got a world of trouble on my mind.
Lookin' for a lover who won't blow my cover,
She's so hard to find.
(To Chorus:)

Ventura Highway

Key Thoughts

"Ventura Highway" was the lead-off track on America's 1973 release, *Homecoming*. Dewey Bunnell wrote the song, and he sang the lead and played rhythm guitar on the recording, while Dan Peek and Gerry Beckley played the signature licks throughout. Joining the trio for this record were temporary bassist Joe Osborn and legendary session drummer Hal Blaine.

Take Note

To re-create the sound on the lush original recording of "Ventura Highway," you'll need *three* acoustic guitars. If you play with two other guitarists—great, you've got it covered. Otherwise, you'll have to adapt the parts to fit your situation. If you play with one other guitarist, the lead player should play Gtr. 1's part and the rhythm player should play Gtr. 3's part. You might miss Gtr. 2 a little, but you won't miss it as much as you'd miss Gtr. 1. That's because Gtr. 1 plays the lead melody, while Gtr. 2 plays *harmony*.

It's difficult to emulate the recording as a solo guitarist, but you can approximate it by alternating between Gtr. 1 and Gtr. 3 throughout the intro. For instance, play Gtr. 1's part for measure 1, then slide down and pick up the rhythm of Gtr. 3's part as quickly as you can. As you reach the end of measure 2, leave out the last strum (or two) so that you can pop up to play Gtr. 1's part in measure 3. For the verse, just stick to the rhythm, and you'll have a much easier time singing the melody.

DEFINITION

When you play **harmony** to another part, you're playing a complementary part. Many harmony guitar parts follow the same contour as the corresponding melody, and they often use intervals of 3rds—like America does in this song—to create the harmonies. (For more on **intervals**, see Appendix A: Chord Theory.)

Fill Variation 1

Fill Variation 2

![FUN FACT icon] **FUN FACT**

In an interview with the *Los Angeles Times* in 2006, Dewey Bunnell said, "It was 1963 when I was in seventh grade, we got a flat tire, and we're standing on the side of the road and I was staring at this highway sign. It said 'Ventura' on it and it just stuck with me. It was a sunny day and the ocean there, all of it." Regarding the lyrics, "Seasons crying no despair, alligator lizards in the air," Bunnell said, "The clouds. It's my brother and I standing there on the side of the road looking at the shapes of clouds while my dad changed the tire."

The road Dewey was on is actually the Ventura Freeway. There is no Ventura Highway, but thanks to the uplifting, optimistic feeling of the song, we can all picture ourselves cruising along an idyllic Ventura road winding along the Pacific Coast on a beautiful summer day.

Ventura Highway

Words and Music by
DEWEY BUNNELL

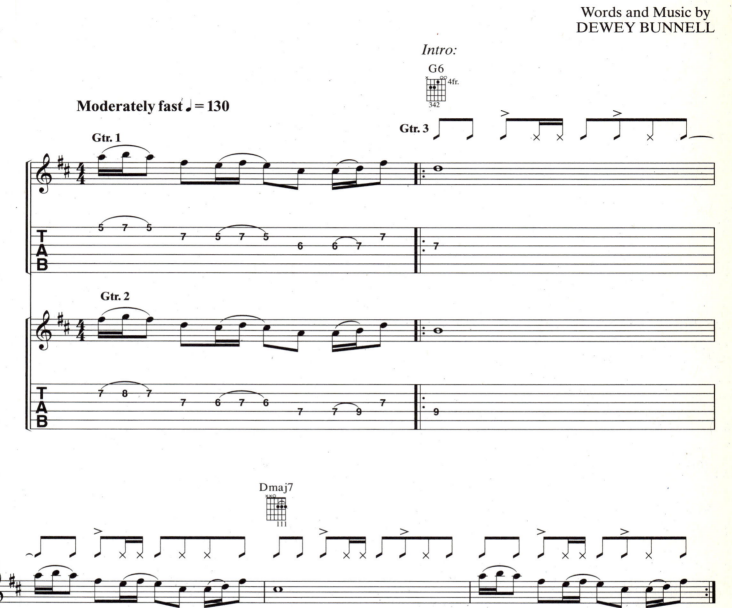

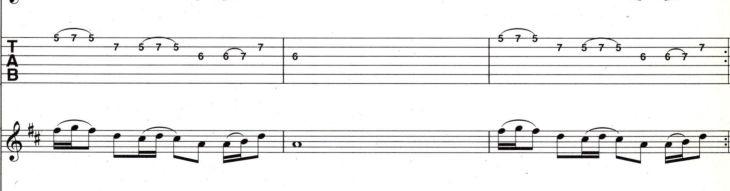

Verse 2:
Wishin' on a fallin' star,
Watchin' for the early train.
Sorry, boy, but I've been hit by purple rain.
Aw, come on, Joe,
You can always change your name.
Thanks, a lot, son, just the same.
(To Chorus:)

Wish You Were Here

Pink Floyd was the ultimate psychedelic band, masterfully weaving continuous soundscapes into complete concept albums like *Dark Side of the Moon* and *Wish You Were Here*. Despite the band's focus on concept records, they included at least a few individual songs on each album that could stand on their own. The title track to *Wish You Were Here* is one of those songs—a tune so popular that its instantly recognizable intro riff has become a favorite guitar-testing tool in music stores all over the world.

Take Note

The signature intro riff uses hammer-on notes and several walking bass lines that give the simple chord progression the trademark Pink Floyd sound. Notice how all of these chords share the same two notes on the top two strings. Not only does this sound great, but it allows you to navigate easily through the shapes with your ring and pinky fingers in the same place throughout the chord progression. The down-stemmed notes in the transcription show the bass line, while the up-stemmed notes show the chordal strums played in between. Play all of this with a pick, letting the bass notes and strums ring out for their full value.

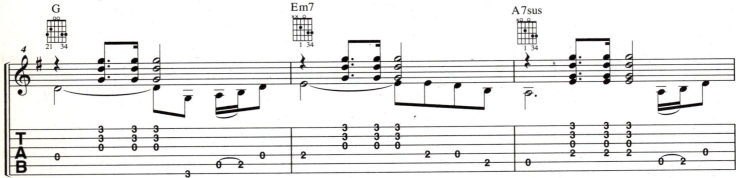

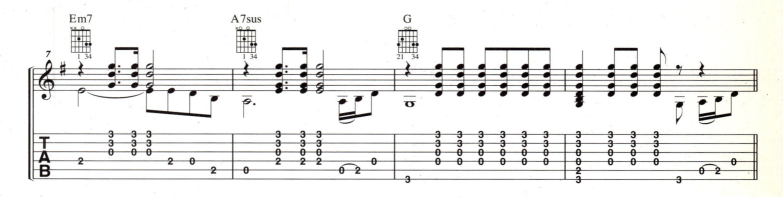

Over the top of the riff in measures 1–5, guitarist David Gilmour uses slides, hammer-ons, and pull-offs to craft a lead line with notes from the G major pentatonic scale.

The G major pentatonic scale.

In measure 5, Gilmour begins to carefully add several notes to his G major pentatonic scale. The bends up to C♯ in measure 6 sound great, even though C♯ is not part of that scale (or most other G scales). But C♯ *is* a chord tone of an A chord—the background chord at this point—and that's why this note sounds good here. In measures 5 and 7, he adds one more note—F♯—which comes from a regular G major scale (G–A–B–C–D–E–F♯).

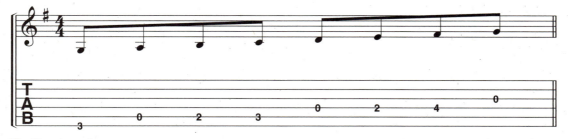

The G major scale.

FUN FACT

"Wish You Were Here" was written about original Pink Floyd songwriter and member Syd Barrett. Barrett was the creative spark behind Pink Floyd's early music, but he left the group in 1968 amid rumors of mental illness.

GUITAR GODS

PINK FLOYD's David Gilmour isn't one of the flashier guitarists, but his subtle and tasteful parts and solos are some of the most memorable classic rock moments. His bluesy, understated approach on "Wish You Were Here" and "Another Brick in the Wall (Part II)" continues to inspire guitarists of all ages.

Wish You Were Here

Words and Music by
ROGER WATERS and DAVID GILMOUR

Slow ♩ = 60 % *Intro:*

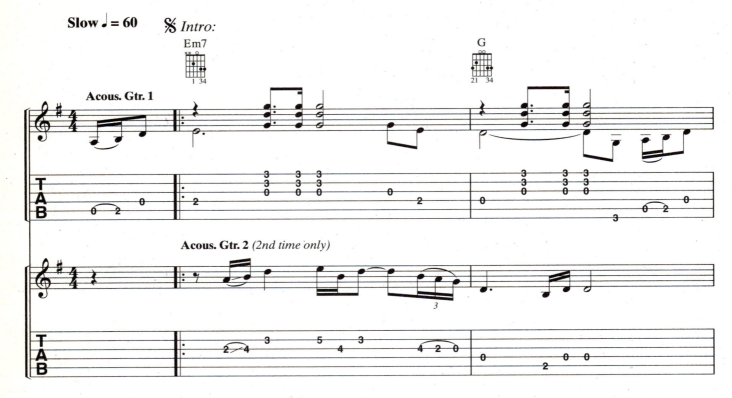

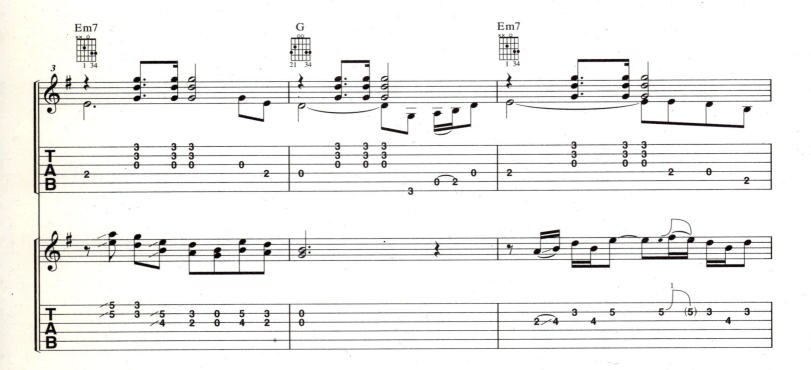

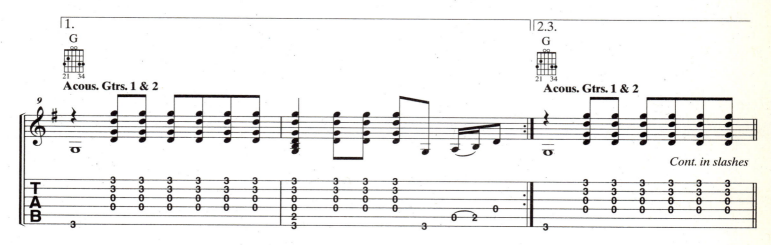

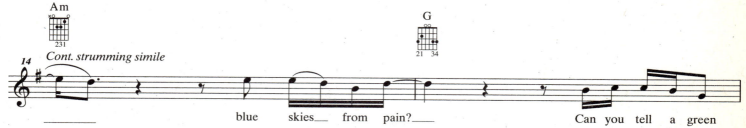

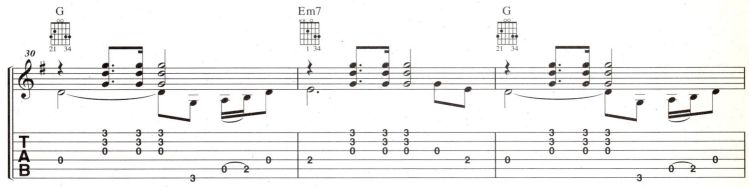

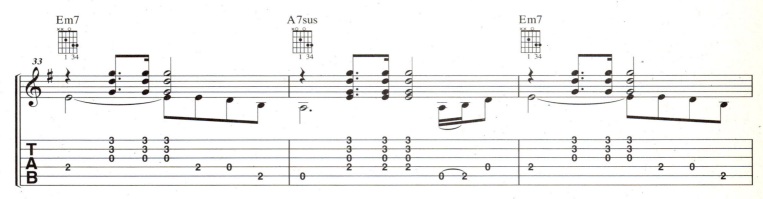

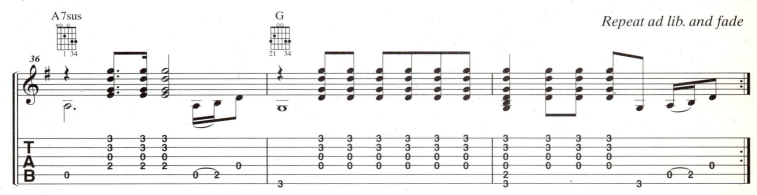

Verse 2:
How I wish,
How I wish you were here.
We're just two lost souls
Swimming in a fish bowl,
Year after year.
Running over the same ground,
What have we found?
The same old fears,
Wish you were here.

Chord Theory

You don't have to understand the music theory of chord construction to play the songs in this book. The notation, TAB, and chord diagrams tell you everything you need to know to play the music correctly. Someday, though, you're bound to find music that doesn't give you as much information as we have, and you'll need to know at least a little bit about chords to get it right. This section should help you out in those situations, and also add some basic chops to your knowledge of music.

Intervals

Play any note on the guitar, then play a note one fret above it. The distance between these two notes is a *half step*. Play another note followed by a note two frets above it. The distance between these notes is a *whole step* (two half steps). The distance between any two notes is referred to as an *interval*.

In the example of the C major scale on the following page, the letter names are shown above the notes, and the *scale degrees* (numbers) of the notes are written below. Notice that C is the first degree of the scale, D is the second, and so on.

The name of an interval is determined by counting the number of scale degrees from one note to the next. For example, an interval of a 3rd, starting on C, would be determined by counting up three scale degrees, or C–D–E (1–2–3). C to E is a 3rd. An interval of a 4th, starting on C, would be determined by counting up four scale degrees, or C–D–E–F (1–2–3–4). C to F is a 4th.

Intervals are not only labeled by the distance between scale degrees, but by the *quality* of the interval. An interval's quality is determined by counting the number of whole steps and half steps between the two notes of that interval. For example, C to E is a 3rd. C to E is also a *major* 3rd because there are 2 whole steps between C and E. Likewise, C to E♭ is a 3rd. C to E♭ is also a *minor* third because there are 1½ steps between C and E♭.

There are five qualities used to describe intervals: *major, minor, perfect, diminished,* and *augmented*.

Interval Qualities

Quality	Abbreviation
major	M
minor	m
perfect	P
diminished	dim or °
augmented	aug or +

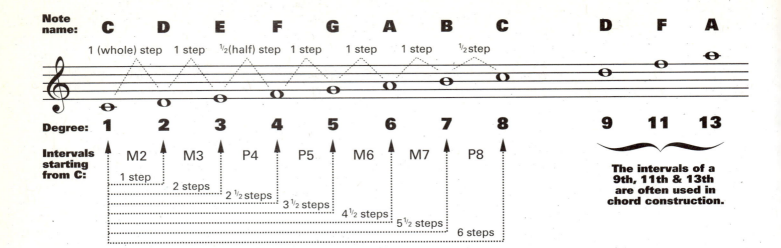

Particular intervals are associated with certain qualities. Not all qualities pertain to every type of interval, as seen in the following table.

Interval Type	Possible Qualities
2nd, 9th	major, minor, augmented
3rd, 6th, 13th	major, minor, diminished, augmented
4th, 5th, 11th	perfect, diminished, augmented
7th	major, minor, diminished

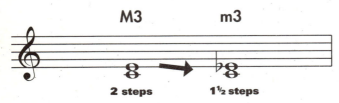

When a major interval is made smaller by a half step, it becomes a minor interval.

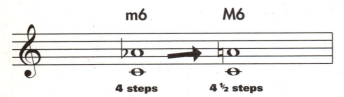

When a minor interval is made larger by a half step, it becomes a major interval.

When a perfect or minor interval is made smaller by a half step, it becomes a diminished interval.

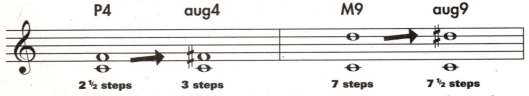

When a perfect or major interval is made larger by a half step, it becomes an augmented interval.

Following is a table of intervals starting on the note C. Notice that some intervals are labeled *enharmonic*, which means that they are written differently but sound the same (see aug2 and m3).

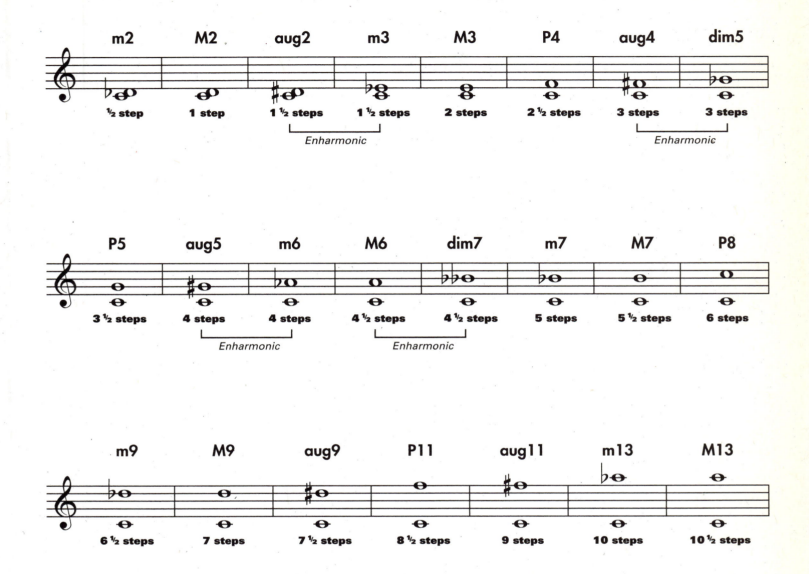

Basic Triads

Two or more notes played together are called a *chord*. Most commonly, a chord will consist of three or more notes. A three-note chord is called a *triad*. The *root* of a triad (or any other chord) is the note from which a chord is constructed. The relationship of the intervals from the root to the other notes of a chord determines the chord *type*. Triads are most frequently identified as one of four chord types: *major*, *minor*, *diminished*, and *augmented*.

Chord Types

All chord types can be identified by the intervals used to create the chord. For example, the C major triad is built beginning with C as the root, adding a major 3rd (E) and adding a perfect 5th (G). All major triads contain a root, M3, and P5.

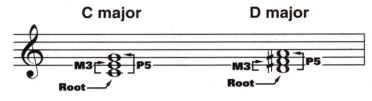

Minor triads contain a root, minor 3rd, and perfect 5th. (An easier way to build a minor triad is to simply lower the 3rd of a major triad.) All minor triads contain a root, m3, and P5.

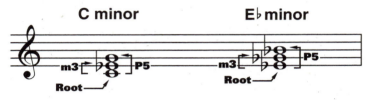

Diminished triads contain a root, minor 3rd, and diminished 5th. If the perfect 5th of a minor triad is made smaller by a half step (to become a diminished 5th), the result is a diminished triad. All diminished triads contain a root, m3, and dim5.

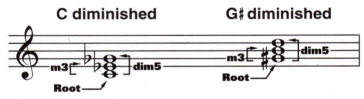

Augmented triads contain a root, major 3rd, and augmented 5th. If the perfect 5th of a major triad is made larger by a half step (to become an augmented 5th), the result is an augmented triad. All augmented triads contain a root, M3, and aug5.

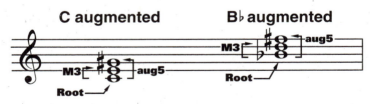

Chord Inversions

An important concept to remember about chords is that the bottom note of a chord will not always be the root. If the root of a triad, for instance, is moved above the 5th so that the 3rd is the bottom note of the chord, it is said to be in the *first inversion*. If the root and 3rd are moved above the 5th, the chord is in the *second inversion*. The number of inversions that a chord can have is related to the number of notes in the chord: a three-note chord can have two inversions, a four-note chord can have three inversions, etc.

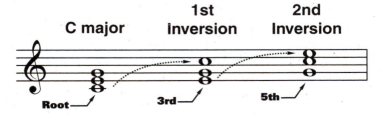

Building Chords

By using the four chord types as basic building blocks, it is possible to create a variety of chords by adding 6ths, 7ths, 9ths, 11ths, and so on. The following are examples of some of the many variations.

C Major Suspended Fourth
Csus

C Flat Fifth
C(♭5)
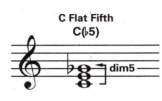

C Major Add Ninth
C(add9)

C Diminished
C°

C Major Sixth
C6
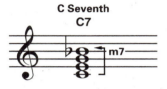

C Sixth Add Ninth
C6/9
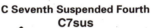

C Minor Sixth Add Ninth
Cm6/9
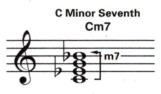

C Minor Sixth
Cm6
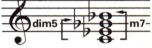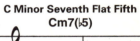

C Seventh
C7
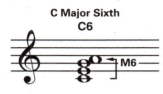

C Seventh Suspended Fourth
C7sus

C Minor Seventh
Cm7

C Minor Seventh Flat Fifth
Cm7(♭5)
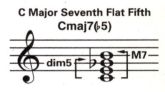

C Seventh Augmented Fifth
C7+
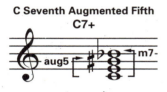

C Seventh Flat Fifth
C7(♭5)
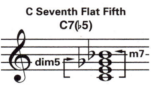

C Major Seventh
Cmaj7
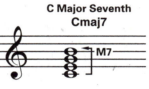

C Major Seventh Flat Fifth
Cmaj7(♭5)
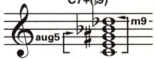

C Minor Major Seventh
Cm(maj7)

C Seventh Flat Ninth
C7(♭9)
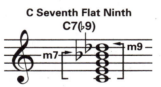

C Seventh Augmented Ninth
C7(♯9)
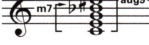

C Seventh Flat Ninth Augmented Fifth
C7+(♭9)
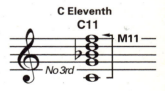

C Minor Ninth
Cm9
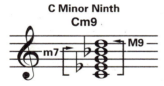

C Ninth
C9
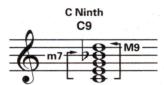

C Ninth Augmented Fifth
C9+
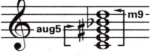

C Ninth Flat Fifth
C9(♭5)

C Major Ninth
Cmaj9
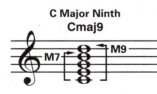

C Ninth Augmented Eleventh
C9(♯11)
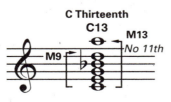

C Minor Ninth Major Seventh
Cm9(maj7)
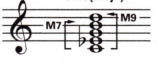

C Eleventh
C11
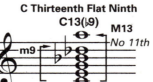

C Minor Eleventh
Cm11
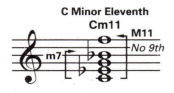

C Thirteenth
C13

C Thirteenth Flat Ninth
C13(♭9)

C Thirteenth Flat Ninth Flat Fifth
C13(♭9♭5)

So far, the examples provided to illustrate intervals and chord construction have been based on C. Until you're familiar with chords, the C chord examples on the previous page can serve as a guide for building chords based on other notes. For example, to construct a G7(♭9) chord, you can first determine what intervals are contained in C7(♭9) and use the steps below to build the same chord starting on G.

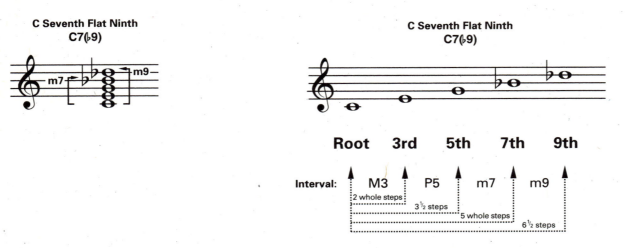

- First, determine the *root* of the chord. A chord is always named for its root, so G is the root of G7(♭9).

- Count *letter names* up from the *letter name of the root* (G) to determine the intervals of the chord. Counting three letter names up from G to B (G–A–B, 1–2–3) is a 3rd, G to D (G–A–B–C–D) is a 5th, G to F is a 7th, and G to A is a 9th.

- Determine the *quality* of the intervals by counting half steps and whole steps up from the root. G to B (2 whole steps) is a major 3rd, G to D (3½ steps) is a perfect 5th, G to F (5 whole steps) is a minor 7th, and G to A♭ (6½ steps) is a minor 9th.

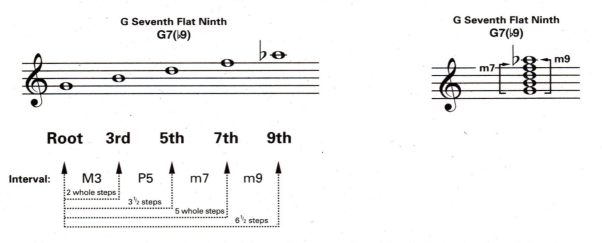

Follow this general guideline for determining the notes of any chord. As intervals and chord construction become more familiar to you, you'll be able to create original fingerings on the guitar. Don't be afraid to experiment!

The Circle of Fifths

The *circle of fifths* will help to clarify which chords are enharmonic equivalents (yes, chords can be written enharmonically as well as notes). The circle of fifths also serves as a quick reference guide to the relationship of the keys and how key signatures can be figured out in a logical manner. Moving clockwise (up a P5) provides all of the sharp keys by progressively adding one sharp to the key signature. Moving counter-clockwise (down a P5) provides the flat keys by progressively adding one flat to the key signature.

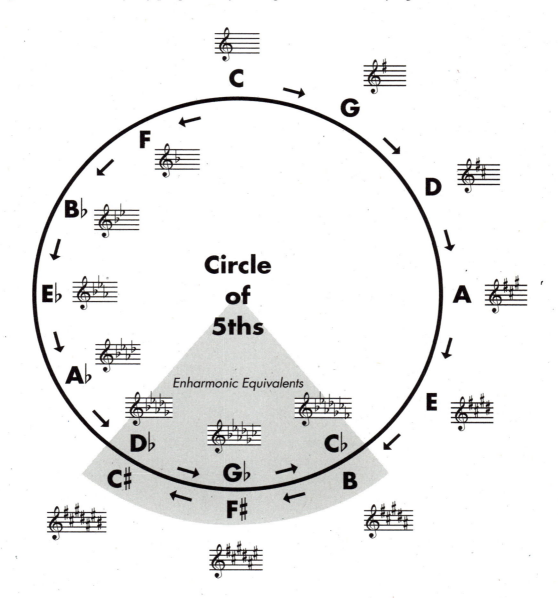

Chord Symbol Variations

Chord symbols are a form of musical shorthand that provide you with as much information about a chord as quickly as possible. The intent of using chord symbols is to convey enough information to recognize the chord, yet not so much as to confuse the meaning of the symbol. Chord symbols are not universally standardized and are written in many different ways—some are easy to understand, others are confusing. To illustrate this point, following is a list of some of the variations copyists, composers, and arrangers have created for the more common chord symbols.

C	**Csus**	**C($\flat$5)**	**C(add9)**	**C5**	**Cm**
C major	Csus4	C-5	C(9)	C(no3)	Cmin
Cmaj	C(addF)	C(5-)	C(add2)	C(omit3)	Cmi
CM	C4	C($\sharp$4)	C(+9)		C-
			C(+D)		

C+	**C°**	**C6**	**C6/9**	**Cm6/9**	**Cm6**
C+5	Cdim	Cmaj6	C6(add9)	C-6/9	C-6
Caug	Cdim7	C(addA)	C6(addD)	Cm6(+9)	Cm(addA)
Caug5	C7dim	C(A)	C9(no7)	Cm6(add9)	Cm(+6)
C($\sharp$5)			C9/6	Cm6(+D)	

C7	**C7sus**	**Cm7**	**Cm7($\flat$5)**	**C7+**	**C7($\flat$5)**
C(addB$\flat$)	C7sus4	Cmi7	Cmi7-5	C7+5	C7-5
C$\overline{7}$	Csus7	Cmin7	C-7(5-)	C7aug	C7(5-)
C(-7)	C7(+4)	C-7	C$\varnothing$	C7aug5	C$\overline{7}$-5
C(+7)		C7mi	C ½dim	C7($\sharp$5)	C7($\sharp$4)

Cmaj7	**Cmaj7($\flat$5)**	**Cm(maj7)**	**C7($\flat$9)**	**C7($\sharp$9)**	**C7+($\flat$9)**
Cma7	Cmaj7(-5)	C-maj7	C7(-9)	C7(+9)	Caug7-9
C$\overline{7}$	C$\overline{7}$(-5)	C-$\overline{7}$	C9$\flat$	C9$\sharp$	C+7($\flat$9)
C$\triangle$	C$\triangle$($\flat$5)	Cmi$\overline{7}$	C9-	C9+	C+9$\flat$
C$\triangle$7					C7+(-9)

Cm9	**C9**	**C9+**	**C9($\flat$5)**	**Cmaj9**	**C9($\sharp$11)**
Cm7(9)	C$^9_7$	C9(+5)	C9(-5)	C$\overline{7}$(9)	C9(+11)
Cm7(+9)	C7add9	Caug9	C7$^9_{5}$	C$\overline{7}$(+9)	C($\sharp$11)
C-9	C7(addD)	C($\sharp$9$\sharp$5)	C9(5$\flat$)	C9(maj7)	C11+
Cmi7(9+)	C7(+9)	C+9		C$\overline{9}$	C11$\sharp$

Cm9(maj7)	**C11**	**Cm11**	**C13**	**C13($\flat$9)**	**C13($^{\flat 9}_{\flat 5}$)**
C-9($\sharp$7)	C9(11)	C-11	C9addA	C13(-9)	C13(-9-5)
C(-9)$\overline{7}$	C9addF	Cm($\flat$11)	C9(6)	C$^{13}_{\flat 9}$	C($\flat$9$\flat$5)addA
Cmi9($\sharp$7)	C9+11	Cmi7$^{11}_{9}$	C7addA	C($\flat$9)addA	
	C7$^9_{11}$	C-7($^9_{11}$)	C7+A		

Reading Chord Frames

Guitar chord frames are diagrams that show the fingering and position of a particular chord on the neck of the guitar. Vertical lines represent the strings, and horizontal lines represent the frets. Dots on the diagram show exactly where to place the fingers, and corresponding numbers at the bottom of the frame tell which fingers to use.

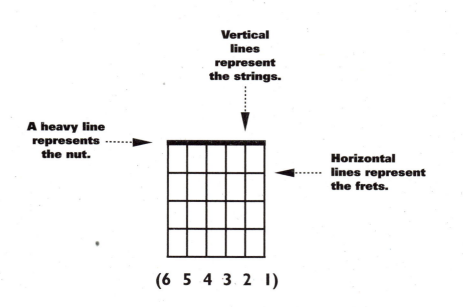

Vertical lines represent the strings.

A heavy line represents the nut.

Horizontal lines represent the frets.

(6 5 4 3 2 1)

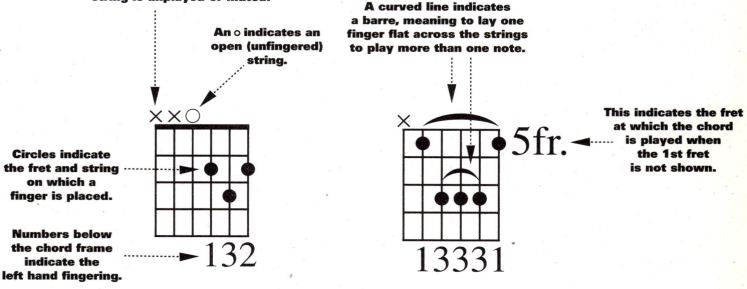

An X indicates that the string is unplayed or muted.

An o indicates an open (unfingered) string.

A curved line indicates a barre, meaning to lay one finger flat across the strings to play more than one note.

This indicates the fret at which the chord is played when the 1st fret is not shown.

Circles indicate the fret and string on which a finger is placed.

Numbers below the chord frame indicate the left hand fingering.

132

5fr.

13331

Guitar
Fingerboard Chart

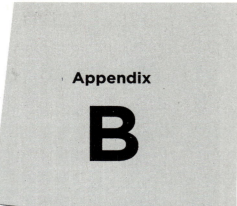

Appendix

B

Frets 1–12

STRINGS

6th	5th	4th	3rd	2nd	1st
E	A	D	G	B	E

FRETS / STRINGS

FRETS	6th	5th	4th	3rd	2nd	1st
Open	E	A	D	G	B	E
1st Fret	F	A#/B♭	D#/E♭	G#/A♭	C	F
2nd Fret	F#/G♭	B	E	A	C#/D♭	F#/G♭
3rd Fret	G	C	F	A#/B♭	D	G
4th Fret	G#/A♭	C#/D♭	F#/G♭	B	D#/E♭	G#/A♭
5th Fret	A	D	G	C	E	A
6th Fret	A#/B♭	D#/E♭	G#/A♭	C#/D♭	F	A#/B♭
7th Fret	B	E	A	D	F#/G♭	B
8th Fret	C	F	A#/B♭	D#/E♭	G	C
9th Fret	C#/D♭	F#/G♭	B	E	G#/A♭	C#/D♭
10th Fret	D	G	C	F	A	D
11th Fret	D#/E♭	G#/A♭	C#/D♭	F#/G♭	A#/B♭	D#/E♭
12th Fret	E	A	D	G	B	E

Fretboard diagram (strings 6th 5th 4th 3rd 2nd 1st = E A D G B E):

Fret	6th	5th	4th	3rd	2nd	1st
1st	F	A# / B♭	D# / E♭	G# / A♭	C	F
2nd	F# / G♭	B	E	A	C# / D♭	F# / G♭
3rd	G	C	F	A# / B♭	D	G
4th	G# / A♭	C# / D♭	F# / G♭	B	D# / E♭	G# / A♭
5th	A	D	G	C	E	A
6th	A# / B♭	D# / E♭	G# / A♭	C# / D♭	F	A# / B♭
7th	B	E	A	D	G♭	B
8th	C	F	A# / B♭	D# / E♭	G	C
9th	C# / D♭	F# / G♭	B	E	A♭	C# / D♭
10th	D	G	C	F	A	D
11th	D# / E♭	G# / A♭	C# / D♭	F# / G♭	A# / B♭	D# / E♭
12th	E	A	D	G	B	E

Glossary

accent   Emphasis on a beat, note, or chord.

accidental   A sharp, flat, or natural sign that occurs in a measure.

altered tuning   Any tuning other than standard tuning on the guitar.

arpeggio   The notes of a chord played one after another instead of simultaneously.

backbeats   In $\frac{4}{4}$ time, beats 2 and 4 in a measure. In most types of rock and pop music, the drummer usually accents the backbeats by hitting the snare, giving the music a strong feeling of forward momentum.

bar   See *measure (or bar)*.

bar line   A vertical line that indicates where one measure ends and another begins.

barre   To fret multiple strings with one finger.

barre chord   A chord played by fretting several strings with one finger.

bend   A technique of pushing a guitar string up or down with the fretting finger to change the pitch.

bridge   The part of the guitar that anchors the strings to the body.

brush stroke   To lightly strum the guitar strings with the index finger of the right hand.

capo   A device placed around the neck of the guitar to raise the pitch of the strings.

Carter style   A guitar technique, named after Maybelle Carter of the Carter Family, that combines rhythm strumming and single-note melody playing.

chord   A group of three or more notes played simultaneously.

chord progression   A sequence of chords played in succession.

common time   The most common time signature found in music; there are four beats to every measure and the quarter note gets one beat. Same as $\frac{4}{4}$.

countermelody   A melody played at the same time as the main melody.

cut time   A time signature that usually indicates a faster tempo where there are two beats to every measure and the half note gets one beat. Same as $\frac{2}{2}$.

dotted note   A note followed by a dot, indicating that the length of the note is longer by one half of the note's original length.

double bar line   A sign made of one thin line and one thick line, indicating the end of a piece of music.

double drop D tuning   An altered tuning in which both the 1st and 6th strings of the guitar are lowered from E to D.

double stop   A group of two notes played simultaneously.

downbeat   The first beat of a measure.

down-pick   To pick the string downward, toward the floor.

down-stroke   To strike the strings downward, toward the floor.

down-strum   To strum the strings downward, toward the floor.

drop D tuning   An altered tuning in which the 6th string of the guitar is lowered from E to D.

economy of motion   A concept for efficient playing that involves moving as few fingers as little as possible when changing chords.

eighth note   A note equal to half a quarter note, or one half beat in $\frac{4}{4}$ time.

eighth rest   A rest equal to the duration of an eighth note.

enharmonic   Two notes of the same pitch, but with different names. For example, B♭ and A♯ are enharmonic notes.

fermata   A symbol that indicates to hold a note for about twice as long as usual.

fifth   The 5th note of a scale above the root note, the distance of seven half steps.

fingerboard   See *fretboard*.

fingerpicking   A style of playing that uses the right hand fingers to pluck the guitar strings rather than using a pick.

fingerstyle   To play the strings with the fingers rather than with a pick.

flat   A symbol that indicates to lower a note one half step.

fret   The metal strips across the fretboard of a guitar.

fretboard   The part of the guitar neck where the frets lay.

G clef   See *treble clef*.

grace note   A small note played quickly either just before a beat or right on the beat.

groove   The sense of rhythm in a piece of music.

half note   A note equal to two quarter notes, or two beats in $\frac{4}{4}$ time.

half rest   A rest equal to the duration of a half note.

half step   The distance of one fret on the guitar.

hammer-on   A technique by which a note is made to sound after playing the string with the right hand by tapping down on the string with another finger of the fretting hand.

harmonics   The notes of the harmonic series that sound clear and bell-like when played, produced by lightly touching a string at various points on the fretboard and indicated in notation with diamond-shaped symbols.

harmony   The result of two or more tones played simultaneously.

interval   The distance in pitch between notes.

key   The tonal center of a piece of music.

key signature   The group of sharps or flats that appears at the beginning of a piece of music to indicate what key the music is in.

ledger lines   Short horizontal lines used to extend a staff either higher or lower.

major chord   A chord consisting of a root, a major 3rd, and a perfect 5th.

major scale   The most common scale in music, consisting of a specific order of whole and half steps: W–W–H–W–W–W–H.

major third   A note that is four half steps up from the root.

measure (or bar)   Divisions of the staff that are separated by bar lines and contain equal numbers of beats.

minor chord   A chord consisting of a root, a minor 3rd, and a perfect 5th.

minor third   A note that is three half steps up from the root.

mode   A set of notes arranged into a specific scale.

mute   To stop a note from ringing on the guitar by placing either the right or left hand over the strings.

natural   A symbol that indicates a note is not sharp or flat.

note   A symbol used to represent a musical tone.

nut   The part of the guitar at the top of the neck that aligns the strings over the fretboard.

octave   The interval between two immediate notes of the same name, equivalent to 12 frets on the guitar, or eight scale steps.

open E tuning   An altered tuning for the guitar in which the strings are tuned from low to high E–B–E–G♯–B–E.

open position   Fingering for chords that incorporates open strings and no barre.

palm mute   A technique of muffling the guitar strings with the right hand palm at the bridge of the guitar.

pendulum strumming   A technique in which you keep your arm moving up and down even if a strum is not indicated. The idea is keep a strong groove by not breaking strumming momentum.

pick   A device used to pluck or strum the strings of a guitar.

pima   Abbreviations for the right hand fingers in fingerpicking notation, in which p = thumb, i = index finger, m = middle finger, and a = ring finger.

pinch technique   A fingerpicking technique in which the right hand plucks two strings at once between the thumb and another finger.

pitch   The location of a note related to its lowness or highness.

position   The location of the hand on the fretboard at a particular fret.

pull-off   A left hand technique in which two notes are fingered on the same string, and the lower note is then made to sound by pulling the fretting finger off the higher note.

quarter note   A note equal to one beat in $\frac{4}{4}$ time and the basic unit of musical time.

quarter rest   A rest equal to the duration of a quarter note.

repeat signs   A group of various symbols indicating sections of music to be played over again.

rest   A symbol representing measured silence in music.

rhythm   The musical organization of beats.

riff   A short, repeated melodic pattern.

root note   The fundamental note of a chord, and also the note that gives the chord its letter name. The root is the first note of the corresponding major scale.

scale   A set of notes arranged in a specific order of whole steps and half steps. The most common scale is the major scale.

sharp   A symbol that indicates to raise a note one half step.

shuffle rhythm   A rhythm in which eighth notes are played in an uneven, long-short manner.

sixteenth note   A note equal to half an eighth note, or one quarter beat in $\frac{4}{4}$ time.

sixteenth rest   A rest equal to the duration of a sixteenth note.

slash chord   A chord with a note other than the root in the bass. These are labeled with the chord name on the left, followed by a slash with the bass note listed to the right.

slide 1: A technique of moving smoothly from one note to another. A note is fingered by the left hand and played by the right hand, then the left hand finger maintains pressure while sliding quickly on the string to the next note without interrupting the sound or picking the note again. Indicated in notation with a diagonal line between notes. 2: A metal or glass tubing that fits over a left hand finger, used to fret the strings and produce slide notes.

staccato To play notes in a short, detached manner. Indicated in notation by a dot directly over or under the note or chord.

staff The horizontal lines and spaces upon which music notes are placed to designate their pitch.

standard tuning The normal tuning for the guitar in which the strings are tuned from low to high E–A–D–G–B–E.

strum To play several strings by brushing quickly across them with a pick or the fingers.

swing To play eighth notes in an uneven, long-short rhythm.

syncopation A shift of rhythmic emphasis to the weak beat, or to a weak part of a beat.

TAB Abbreviation for *tablature*.

tablature A system of guitar notation that uses a graphic representation of the six strings of the guitar with numbers indicating which fret to play.

tempo The speed at which music is played.

tie A curved line that joins two or more notes of the same pitch, indicating to play them as one continuous note.

time signature A sign resembling a fraction that appears at the beginning of a piece of music. The top number indicates how many beats are in each measure and the bottom number indicates what kind of note gets one beat.

Travis picking A picking technique, named for country guitarist Merle Travis, in which the right thumb plays constant notes alternating between two strings.

treble clef A symbol at the beginning of the staff that designates the second line as the note G. Also called the *G clef.*

triplet A group of three notes played in the time of two.

unison The same pitch played at the same time on different strings of the guitar.

up-pick To pick the string upward, toward the ceiling.

up-stroke To strike the strings upward, toward the ceiling.

up-strum To strum the strings upward, toward the ceiling.

whole note A note equal to four quarter notes, or four beats in $\frac{4}{4}$ time.

whole rest A rest equal to the duration of a whole note, or the duration of any full measure.

whole step The distance of two frets on the guitar.

The following blank chord frames may be used to keep track of new chords. Write them here as you learn so you won't forget them.

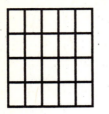
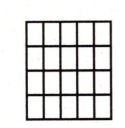
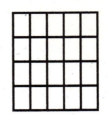
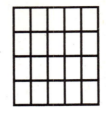

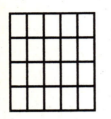
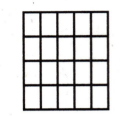
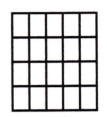
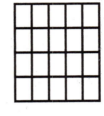

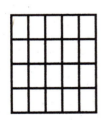
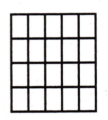

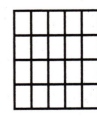